All royalties generated from sales of this book will be paid to the Sir Patrick Geddes Memorial Trust.

Think Global, Act Local

The Life and Legacy of Patrick Geddes

WALTER STEPHEN

SOFIA LEONARD

MURDO MACDONALD

KENNETH MACLEAN

NARAYANI GUPTA

Luath Press Limited

EDINBURGH

www.luath.co.uk

First published 2004

The paper used in this book is recyclable. It is made from
low chlorine pulps produced in a low energy, low emission manner
from renewable forests.

Printed and bound by
Digisource (GB) Ltd., Livingston

Typeset in 10.5 point Sabon by
S. Fairgrieve, Edinburgh 0131 658 1763

'Well, you will probably think me considerably more plain than pleasant in my remarks.'

'So beyond working and playing comes remembering, in some ways the happiest of all.'

'Our Edinburgh legal idea of business (is one) which eliminates all considerations of feeling, individual or public, which attains the ideal of utmost coldness to all, thus coinciding with the lowest circle of the Inferno – that of Ice. For your own sake and that of others, why stay there?'

'There is no permanent reason for men to kill each other... Give them hope of a better land, of enough food for their families, and you remove a main cause of bloodshed.'

'The child's desire of seeing and hearing, touching and handling, of smelling and tasting are all true and healthy hungers, and it can hardly be too strongly insisted that good teaching begins, neither with knowledge nor discipline, but through delight.'

'I can't and won't keep accounts!'

'Since the Industrial Revolution, there has gone on an organised sacrifice of men to things, a large-scale subordination of life to machinery.'

'Best way too of aiding the great causes – national, European, human – for which our sons have died is to take our share in preparing others to live further.'

'The healthy curiosity of an intelligent child can always puzzle all the Doctors of the Temple.'

'Town planning is not merely place-planning, nor even work planning. If it is to be successful it must be folk-planning.'

'What was decided among the prehistoric Protozoa cannot be annulled by Act of Parliament.'

'It is but the common urban incapacity to govern agricultural populations, to deal with rustic questions.'

'Those American superiorities which surprise and disconcert old Europe very largely turn, indirectly and directly, upon the superior culture and status of women.'

'While a man can win power over nature, there is magic; while he can stoutly confront life and death, there is romance.'

'Aha! Look at them – how clean and white and useless: the hands of a paper-gentleman.'

'Planning requires long and patient study. The work cannot be done in the office with ruler and parallels, for the plan must be sketched out on the spot, after wearying hours of perambulation.'

'*Pure as a lily* is not really a phrase of hackneyed sham-morals; for it does not mean weak, bloodless, sexless, like your moral philosopher's books, your curate's sermons. The lily's Purity lies in that it has something to be pure; its Glory is in being the most frank and open manifestation of sex in all the organic world.'

PATRICK GEDDES, 1854-1932

Contents

Illustrations – Colour Plates

Illustrations – Figures

Acknowledgements

WALTER STEPHEN HAS AN enormous general acknowledgement to an array of people, living and dead, not least to the authors in the Select Bibliography. The illustrations referred to in the text as Figs 2, 4, and 8 have been used by courtesy of Edinburgh University Library and this kindness is hereby acknowledged.

Murdo Macdonald acknowledges four factors of immediate importance. The first was being introduced to Ninian Stuart by Alastair McIntosh and Verénè Nicolas of the Centre for Human Ecology. The second was becoming more formally involved with issues related to House of Falkland via partnership discussions between the Universities of Dundee and St Andrews, ably convened and facilitated by Laura Meagher. The third was the careful reading of his text by his wife Lorna, which led to significant conceptual expansion. The fourth is his current participation in the 'Learning is Understanding in Practice' project (AHRB funded) in Dundee, to which Geddes's ecological notion of 'by creating we think' becomes ever more relevant.

Kenneth Maclean acknowledges: for general advice and information, particularly about Dr Arthur Geddes, their onetime lecturer, Tom Masterton and Norman Thomson, formerly Heads of Social Subjects, Moray House College of Education; and Dr WM Stephen, former Senior Adviser, Lothian Region. The staff of the Carnegie Library, Dunfermline, for help in tracking down information about Norman Johnson, especially Mrs Dorothy Hall. Access to school log books was made possible by Andrew Dowsie, Archivist, Fife Council, and at Kinglassie Primary School, Miss Nicola Claire, Headteacher and Mrs Christine Sewell, School Secretary. For the drawing of diagrams, Norman Thomson.

Think Global, Act Local
– The Life and Legacy of Patrick Geddes

THE FIRST LINE OF ENQUIRY of the present-day seeker of information is through the search engine to the internet. Keying in the 'Think Global...' mantra the response reads '1 – 10 of 185,000 for Think Global, Act Local'. The manual says that individual search engines search up to a maximum of 17% of the total number of sites on the Web. If this is true it means that there are something like a million references to this simple exhortation whizzing about between the satellites around us – a concept very difficult for this person to seize hold of.

It seems remarkable that such a simple little phrase, almost a truism, should have the power to echo and re-echo around the world. Who are the people who are talking to each other about global thinking and local action, whether or not they are actually acting?

There are scores, no, hundreds of local groups who seem to be concerned about the environment, about sustainable development and about ceasing to be at the mercy of the big battalions, be they political or economic. Thus we have 'Here in East Sussex...', 'Think Global Warming, Act Locally in Pittsburgh', 'Global Citizenship – A Cool Planet for Children', 'Fenland', 'South Sydney Greens', 'Parliamentarians for Global Action'. A Campaign Against the Arms Trade (CAAT) urges us to Think Globally and Act Locally. Various businesses exhort their staff to maintain a focus on being part of a global business environment while adapting to suit the requirements of local markets.

Such a welter of good intentions is unlikely to spring, fully-formed, out of nowhere. Traceable through the documentation is some congruity of timing and purpose. Something significant seems to have occurred around 1992 and the phrase 'local agenda' seems to have surfaced as a catch phrase at the same time. Going back a little further, we find that a World Commission on Environment and Development reported in 1987 and following from this the United Nations' Committee on Environment and Development held an Earth Summit in Rio de Janeiro in 1992.

The outcome of the UN Conference was Agenda 21 – an 'action plan for sustainable development' – forty chapters of guidelines, recommendations and goals. Chapter 28 is, perhaps significantly, the shortest and easiest to understand. Basically, it is an appeal to local authorities to engage in a dialogue about sustainable development with the members of their constituencies. As one commentator said – 'Think global maybe, but act local... the trouble is on our doorstep'. Local authorities were to consult and achieve a consensus with their communities on a 'Local Agenda 21'. There was to be co-operation and coordination internationally and between local authorities. Women and youth were to be involved more in decision-making.

What made Local Agenda 21 special was a clear presumption of change and the rationality of administering change. The action plan would only have been published if the authors had known they were pushing at a half-open door. Thus, if we think of 'Think Global, Act Local', the Rio summit may have been the beginning of its formal recognition, but it was also the culmination of twenty years of slow gestation.

Andrew Jamison, of Aalborg University, has produced a number of models clarifying how environmentalism has developed since the Second World War. In one of these he suggests that an awakening through public education and debate (Phase 1) was eventually followed by stages of professionalisation and internationalisation, with emphases on, respectively, environmental assessment and sustainable development (Phases 4 and 5).

By being the first Secretary-General of the United Nations to be appointed from within that organisation, Kofi Annan is a good example of the professionalisation Jamison describes. Having joined the UN in 1962, Kofi Annan himself has, of course, lived and worked through Jamison's periods of public education and debate, institution building and energy policy definition. He would have been professionally concerned with the debates engendered by the publication of Rachel Carson's *Silent Spring* (1962), the global fuel implications of *Blueprint for Survival* (The Ecologist, 1972), and E F Schumacher's *Small is Beautiful: Economics as if People Mattered* (1974) and had executive responsibilities relating to the oil crisis of 1974.

Taking over in the wake of the Rio summit, in 1997, Kofi Annan must have been as aware as anyone of the mass of public opinion behind its conclusions. By popularising 'Think Global, Act Local' he was demonstrating that, behind the progress of the 1990s, there was a groundswell of twenty or thirty years of activism, but that this in turn was partly a consequence of the thoughts and actions of another who is recorded as having the imagination to coin the phrase in 1915.

Patrick Geddes was born on 2 October 1854, so that this is the 150th anniversary of his birth. His life was long, for his generation – 78 years, and full of variety. He had moments of great exhilaration and sense of achievement, but longer periods of dissatisfaction and frustration with the blind stupidity of his fellow-creatures. He irritated the establishment but scattered ideas around him like a prodigal. 'The gangin fit is aye gettin' goes the old Scots proverb, meaning that it is the active person who is most likely to do well. Geddes proved the opposite. Nobody could have been more active in promoting all sorts of ideas and setting up ways to demonstrate their value, but material success was not the outcome. No matter, for the twentieth century Geddes and his ideas provided a background of humane concern for the betterment of people of all conditions and all races.

Geddes worried constantly about money, but for his causes, not for himself. Geddes was almost like Gandhi, whose material possessions could all be carried in a little cloth bag. In 1973, 41 years after Geddes's death, the Sir Patrick Geddes Memorial Trust was set up to administer what little remained of his estate and two small Funds. To mark the 150th anniversary, the Trust thought it time for a new book on Geddes. Excellent books were published in 1975 (by Paddy Kitchen), 1978 (by Philip Boardman), and 1990 (by Helen Meller) – and the relationship between these dates and the commentary above is no coincidence. However, we think that this is a post-Rio world and it is time to look again at the originator of the text for our times – 'Think Global, Act Local'.

The life of Geddes was complex, interesting and not particularly well organised (or perhaps it was, but in a different way from the rest of us!). One thinks of one of those performers who spin more and more plates – but in the case of Geddes the plates might be in different continents and he did not have the internet. In my contribution to this book, I selectively retell the life of Geddes, trying to separate strands that were in reality always tangled.

No-one could have embodied Scottishness more than Geddes, yet this was mingled with a true internationalism, in theory and in practice. Sofia Leonard has a double advantage over the other contributors. She comes to her understanding of Geddes from an international perspective and a substantial part of her professional life has been spent working with the Geddes legacy. She looks with us at Geddes and his work overseas, recording how her personal search linked with the surviving evidence of his activities.

Murdo Macdonald takes two of Geddes's main concerns, the environment and culture, and examines closely what these meant for Geddes. From his background and upbringing he brought so much. His peers contributed also. Professor Macdonald also assesses the originality of Geddes's own input.

For Kenneth Maclean the interest lies in the survival and dissemination of one of Geddes's main ideas. Geddes talked about Sympathy, Synthesis and Synergy – Sympathy being getting to know the problem, usually by survey (we would call it empathy). Maclean follows the theory and practice of regional survey in our educational system by followers of Geddes to the 1970s.

A Letter from India is just that. In replying to an invitation to attend a symposium in Edinburgh, Narayani Gupta gives us a perspective on Geddes from a country which he loved and for whose people he had great respect. His was Imperial India and he was a European transient. After over fifty years of Independence how is he viewed today from New Delhi?

In 1982 I was fortunate enough to play host to Philip Boardman (American) and two other ex-students of the Collège des Écossais, one Indian, the other Swiss, who had not met for fifty years. Figure 1 shows them looking at photographs of themselves, taken in 1930, printed in Boardman's book (*The Worlds of Patrick Geddes*). The photographs they feature in are the usual 'team photo' taken on semi-ceremonial occasions and, more typically, of Geddes and students in a garden surveying and making notes.

Fig. 1 The Scots College – Fifty Years On

Fifty years since they last met, three former students of the Scots College look at theirselves in Boardman's book. From left to right: Jeannie Geddes (widow of Arthur), Mrs Bharucha, Serge L Gloor (Switzerland), Philip Boardman (United States and Norway), Walter Stephen (Chairman, Sir Patrick Geddes Memorial Trust) and Pheroze R Bharucha (India). *(Scotsman Publications)*

How many of those above are alive today? None of the contributors to this book was alive when Geddes lived. We have had to rely on the evidence of others, from those who knew Geddes and his family, from primary sources, books, articles, maps and plans, and from direct observation of the tangible works of the great man. Given the nature of Geddes and his activities the sources are many and scattered.

Think Global, Act Local is meant to be accessible and easily read and the decision has been taken not to have a text cluttered with references and footnotes. Scholars will, however, want more information than a continuous narrative can give and the contributors wish to acknowledge, in some public way, the help they have received from a wide range of people.

A select bibliography is included at the back of this book. A full bibliography and references will be published on the Sir Patrick Geddes Memorial Trust website at:

www.patrickgeddestrust.co.uk

Walter Stephen, Chairman
Sir Patrick Geddes Memorial Trust

Patrick Geddes – the Life

Walter Stephen

A MILLION VISITORS A year visit Edinburgh Castle, trudging up the Royal Mile to do so. A century ago there were also many visitors, although the experience was much less organised than it is today. Imagine yourself in the Lawnmarket, perhaps just having come up the hill from the Waverley Station, slightly bemused and perhaps a little overawed by the grey tenement blocks all around. Suddenly you are accosted by a man with unruly hair and an intense gaze. Although not unduly tall he appears to dominate the pavement and cobbled street as he begins to talk, and talk, and talk.

He talks about this ancient town of Edinburgh. Like the Pied Piper he leads you up towards the Castle and shows you how the ice moulded an old volcanic plug to provide a defensive site for the ancient settlers. He tells how people were drawn in for security and built a town, with a wall, on the tail of the ridge. He brings to life again the sights and sounds and smells of the growing city and describes the great ones and the colourful pageantry that filled the narrow streets and closes. The tale continues as he shows how the rich and powerful grew tired of their medieval home, where all lived hugger-mugger together, how a plan was made and a New Town begun on the farmland on the other side of the Nor' Loch, how all who could afford it abandoned the Old Town for the New, leaving behind the poor and inadequate. He would show you what he was trying to do to bring back a good life to the Old Town, closes where he and his wife had helped families to clean up and decorate their slums, hostels where university students could live amicably next to tradesmen and craftsmen, new and restored blocks of houses which were luring professional people back to the Old Town for the first time for a century. He might leave you at the Outlook Tower where you could climb to the top floor, look around the Edinburgh region and begin to fit all the pieces together, use the Camera Obscura to survey the area in detail and work your way downstairs, learning about relationships within an ever-widening horizon.

As he made off to engage another group, with your brain reeling and the ideas falling all over each other, you might ask a passer-by 'Who was that?'. With a laugh would come the reply – 'Och, that's jist the Professor'. And this in a city with an ancient University, with a great medical faculty of which the poor knew the strengths and specialisms of most members. Yet this man was not even at Edinburgh, he was a part-time (summer term only) Professor of Biology in University College Dundee, until recently a mere out-station of St Andrews, and not really a proper university at all. Yet he had the common touch and would teach anyone at all about the wonders of their world. He moved easily from city to city, from country to country, from continent to continent, observing, teaching and irritating the complacent. This was Patrick Geddes.

Patrick Geddes was born in Ballater on 2 October 1854, the fourth son of Alexander and Janet Geddes. Patrick's siblings were Robert (born 1839), Jessie (born 1841), John (born 1844) and Alex (born 1846, died 1847). In 1857 the family moved to Mount Tabor, a cottage on Kinnoull Hill, just outside Perth. His parents were forty-six and thirty-nine when Patrick was born, so that he grew up in a household of older parents, whence his brothers had moved on to make their ways in the world. Importantly, this left the developing Patrick as the focus of loving attention by his mother, a big sister like an aunt, and his father, Captain Geddes of the Perthshire Rifles, ex-Sergeant-Major in the Black Watch.

Biographers, and PG himself, are agreed on the significance of Captain Geddes in forming the attitudes which came to characterise the great man. Yet one important background influence has been underestimated, the anomolous social position of his father – an officer who had been promoted from the ranks late in his career.

Enlisting as a drummer, Geddes's father served in the Black Watch at home and in India, rising to the rank of Sergeant-Major and Quartermaster. Three times he was offered a commission and refused but after thirty years service he was put on reserve and commissioned into the Perthshire Rifles as Captain. In a volunteer regiment, his duties would be like those of a Territorial Army officer of today. So he was Captain Geddes, respected for his character and his record, but of doubtful background and certainly with no great financial resources backing him. (The practice of purchasing and selling commissions was not ended until 1871).

Paddy Kitchen, in *A Most Unsettling Person*, shows some surprise when she states that General Paterson, whose daughter Margaret married Robert Geddes, 'thought the Geddes family very small beer'. The Geddes family were small beer. The surprising thing was that the General's daughter was allowed to marry the ex-Quartermaster's son. It must say something for the characters of father, or son, or both, that the wedding took place.

Alexander just missed serving in the Crimea where he might have witnessed the Earl of Cardigan leading the Light Brigade into the Valley of Death, riding out again and back to his private yacht. The same Earl was protected by his family from joining the Army in time for Waterloo and, as Colonel of his regiment, persecuted those officers who had seen real service in India. Although the Highland regiments have always had more of a family atmosphere than the unspeakable Guards and the cavalry, the gap between the son of a shepherd and the sons of Highland lairds was wide. Patrick's father's social position as an Army officer, semi-retired, then retired, could only have been, at best, equivocal. Locally he would have been respected, but not a leader socially – he was, for example, an elder in the Free Kirk, the influence of which Murdo Macdonald deals with at a later stage. But when we take this modest background and lack of influential connections and add PG's notorious refusal to participate in the 'cram-exam' scramble for qualifications, plus his inability to compromise his principles in negotiating with potential sponsors and patrons it is surprising that he managed to achieve anything at all, far less turn the world upside down.

Geddes himself described his childhood as 'growing up in a garden', full of useful produce and abundant with the flowers his mother so loved. His father used the planting of potatoes to give him his first lessons in mathematics. On Sunday afternoons the whole family would walk around examining each plant in detail. Kinnoull Hill was a marvellously rich adventure playground and a viewpoint which stirred the imagination. Edinburgh captivated the young Patrick. Father and son went on long walking tours in the Eastern Highlands during the holidays, storing up observations which would re-emerge in later years in the Valley Section and other models. This writer's own experience of his grandfather, another former Highland soldier who had served in India, was nicknamed 'Binghi' (monkey) and had a vocabulary of Hindi words which he used freely in conversation, suggests that Geddes may have been preconditioned at an early age to a respect for the Indian subcontinent and its peoples.

A plain lifestyle, no exuberant decoration, no highly emotional music, little drama; most of us would regard these as the characteristics of the Free Kirk home and Philip Boardman describes a youth of stern Presbyterianism for the maturing PG. Yet Murdo Macdonald shows us that, however narrow Free Church life in the parishes may have been, the Church was in a ferment of intellectual activity having spun off from a body comprising Scotland's most significant thinkers. The story of its foundation, the Disruption, is one of the great tales of Scottish history and is worth telling again here.

Under the Patronage Act of 1712, parish ministers of the established Church of Scotland were appointed by the local laird, regardless of the wishes of the parishioners. Given the Scottish traditions of secession and egalitarianism it was not surprising that a rumbling of discontent became a rising tide of dissatisfaction. Incredible as it may seem to us today, there was enormous popular interest in the issues around patronage. A Ten Years Conflict came to a head on 18 May 1843, when the General Assembly met in St Andrew's Church in Edinburgh. Something was afoot, 'but calm onlookers believed that a mere few would relinquish their comfortable stipends, their pleasant manses, and present advantages of position... a vast multitude thronged the broad area of George Street, breathlessly awaiting the result and prepared to see the miserable show of eight or ten men voluntarily sacrificing themselves to what was thought a fantastic principle'.

The Moderator read a formal protest, signed by 120 ministers and 72 elders and then 'he left his place, followed first by Dr Chalmers and other prominent men, till the number amounted to four hundred and seventy, who poured forth along the streets, where general astonishment, not unmingled with sorrow, admiration and alarm, prevailed'.

An hour later – news travelled fast in those days! – Lord Jeffrey, former Lord Advocate, said:

'Thank God for Scotland! There is not another country on earth where such a deed could be done'.

In walking out of the Assembly 'all these clergymen, with their families, cast their bread upon the waters, and those who witnessed the dark procession that descended the long steep street towards Tanfield Hall never forgot it'.

(Tanfield Hall is where they formed themselves into 'The General Assembly of the Free Church of Scotland').

These recent dramatic events, so recent that two of Patrick's siblings were young children at the time, must have been gone over time and again at Mount Tabor as the young Patrick learned the importance of principle.

Young Patrick did well at Perth Academy without trying too hard and without deciding what he wanted to do with his life. For a mid-Victorian parent from a military background, Alexander Geddes showed remarkable imagination and tolerance in his dealings with his son, who was bubbling with nervous energy, but had no notion of how to direct it. He had a shed built in the garden for Patrick to carry out chemistry experiments. Patrick was allowed a 'gap year' when he had lessons in cabinetmaking in the mornings, attended the School of Art in the afternoons and was encouraged to read voraciously. (As background to Murdo Macdonald's contribution on Geddes, the environment and culture, it is interesting to note that the mechanical teaching of drawing did not please Geddes, but that he developed some skill as a draughtsman and was always interested in presentation and the use of artistic means for didactic purposes).

In later life, Geddes was to write about Art, its content rather than technique. More importantly, he acted as a patron, commissioning paintings, panels and murals, stained glass for specific locations and usually with a specific message. Like the masons and glaziers of the medieval cathedrals his commissions could be aesthetically satisfying and colourful, but above all they told stories in glass or stone. Fortunate in flourishing at the same time as Art Nouveau, John Duncan and the Celtic Revival, he tried to help the raising of standards by setting up an University Hall School of Art beside the Outlook Tower. The influence of the Free Kirk can be seen in that it was one of Thomas Guthrie's Ragged Schools which Geddes recycled for his art college. (The building awaits redevelopment by the Outlook Tower while Guthrie has his statue in Princes Street Gardens).

Within a few minutes walk of his Edinburgh flat Geddes was responsible for at least the following cultural additions to the Old Town environment, all nice to look at, but laden with symbolism – The Witches' Well on the Castle Esplanade (Plate 1c), decorative additions to several flats and student hostels, murals in his own and other flats, stained glass panels in the Outlook Tower,

Riddle's Court and another of the hostels, the 'modern' painted ceiling in Riddle's Court (Plate 1b). 'Think global, act local' – it is difficult to see how any private citizen without a massive income could have produced so much and so lasting local action in such a short time.

Once again, his father was amazingly tolerant for his time in negotiating with his son on how he might work, as work he must. He tried 'The Bank' for eighteen months and then moved on. In later years Geddes famously said 'I can't and won't keep accounts' and the general impression we have is of financial chaos, permanent cash-flow problems and the incessant pursuit of sponsors and good managers. (Annual running cost of Outlook Tower – £400, annual income – £100 – 'Whaur's your Mr Micawber noo?'). Yet he did well at the bank and his later life saw him wheeling and dealing with the greatest of ease. Paddy Kitchen suggests that he had that kind of facility with money which results from having a low regard for its importance and reminds us that economics was one of the subjects he wrote about!

The next step was to move towards science, and he spent a year in classes in chemistry and geology. Then it was biology. Patrick decided to study at Edinburgh University – and returned home after a week, dissatisfied with the teaching methods! Here is a real problem for the socially responsible biographer. In 1982, on the fiftieth anniversary of PG's death, I was invited to speak to the pupils of Aboyne Academy about this famous native of Deeside (Aboyne being the secondary school Ballater pupils now attend). On the one hand there was this charismatic figure spilling out ideas which were still fresh in 1982, a role model indeed. On the other there was this fellow who had no paper qualifications, never finished anything and never passed an exam (in fact, when at the Royal School of Mines, for a bet and just to show he could do it, he crammed for a week to pass the elementary examination in mining and get a certificate to become a sub-inspector of mines). How could I have these impressionable young souls going home and telling their parents about this world-famous professor, and why did they have to do O Grade Maths if he hadn't?

In some ways Victorian society was more open than ours. Geddes's next move was to the Royal School of Mines (which became the Imperial College of Science in 1907), to study under TH Huxley. Although he had to do a probationary year with the first year students, we must still ask ourselves how a student from a modest provincial background, with amorphous qualifications and no powerful patrons, could be admitted to such august company. Before long, Huxley suggested Geddes start individual research, which resulted in his contradiction of Huxley's findings. Unperturbed, Huxley had Geddes write an illustrated paper which he (Huxley) presented to the Zoological Society as a pupil's correction of his work.

Geddes became a demonstrator in Sanderson's laboratory in University College, London, where he had a lesson demonstrating that greatness could be achieved without any loss of enthusiasm. Geddes was working in the lab 'when he was gently pushed aside. A big beard came over his shoulder – here was Darwin! who had come in unnoticed. He said nothing, but looked closely into this... barren microscope field: then suddenly broke out, positively shouting for joy: 'I say! They're moving! Sanderson! Sanderson! come and see; they're MOVING! look at that!'

Darwin was about seventy at this time and if Geddes needed a model to justify a lifelong persistence and intellectual excitement he now had it.

Huxley next found holiday work for Geddes at a marine biological station in Brittany, at Roscoff. This led to spells at the Sorbonne and Naples, after which Geddes felt ready to apply for university chairs. However, in Paris he met Frederic Le Play from whom he borrowed the concept that societies are affected first by geography and later by occupation. Usually summarised as Place – Work – Folk, this became the foundation of Geddes's own work and beliefs. Surveys were necessary because Folk could only be understood when Work and Place had been thoroughly studied. When Folk chose their Work they could begin to shape their Place according to their needs. In a myriad of contexts the Le Play triad re-emerges as a tool for comprehending the world.

This unsettled career – Geddes was already twenty-seven and appeared to have no plan for moving through life – seemed set to continue when he set off for Mexico, the British Association having granted him £50 to carry out researches in Palaeontology and Zoology. For Geddes to travel to Mexico in October 1879 was not a good move, although, at the time, there seemed good reasons for going there.

Robert, his eldest brother by eighteen years, had started in the bank at Perth. While not particularly happy in his work, he was good at it and eventually became manager of the Land Bank of Mexico in Mexico City. He arrived in a country in turmoil. Taking advantage of the American Civil War, with a resulting lack of interest in events south of the Rio Grande, the French Emperor Napoleon III set up a Mexican empire with Archduke Maximilian, brother of Emperor Franz Joseph of Austria, and his Belgian-born consort, Carlotta, as figureheads. The Confederate surrender at Appomattox meant that the United States could interest itself once again in its Latin American neighbours. Napoleon was persuaded to withdraw his troops, the infant empire collapsed and the unfortunate Maximilian was executed by firing squad, to be famously commemorated by Manet. (Although at that time the leading Impressionist, Manet suffered the indignity of having the public exhibition of the painting forbidden by order of the Emperor Napoleon III).

Although this Imperial interlude was long over by the time Patrick arrived in the country, it could not have escaped his notice that this former Spanish colony had had as undoubted President since 1861 a radical Liberal, a full-blooded Indian called Benito Juarez. Juarez fought off a Conservative challenge to his (constitutional) presidency, successfully led the resistance to the French occupation of his country when Maximilian was forced upon the Mexicans, and reorganised to an acceptable degree post-war Mexico. Geddes must have retained the realisation that Juarez, probably the first democratically elected non-white ruler in the world, was as able as any hidalgo or descendant of the conquistadors to govern in an honest, competent and popular fashion.

However, Mexico was still in some turmoil in 1865 and Robert Geddes had several adventures for which his time in Perth would have left him ill-prepared. Nevertheless, he prospered – his salary starting at £900 per annum had reached £3,000 when he retired at 42 in 1881 (two years after Patrick's sojourn). Patrick would clearly have benefitted from the support his brother could give him in making local contacts, facilitating travel and creating a secure atmosphere for him to work in. Unfortunately, the state of the country was such that he had to be escorted on his field trips and had to return to the city every night.

Catastrophe struck PG when he fell seriously ill and lost his sight. For anyone this is an appalling thing to happen. For Geddes, to whom sight was so important a part of his professional life as he peered down into the microscope, it must have been extreme. All we know about him suggests that sight was vital to his everyday existence – the view from Kinnoull Hill, the miracle of the diversity of life forms, the colour of the Mediterranean soils.

Geddes was not the first to suffer sensory loss at the height of his powers. There is no more tragic document to read than the so-called 'Heiligenstadt Testament', in which Beethoven reached extremes of misery as he realised that he was losing the supreme gift that marked him out from the rest of the world.

In the middle of the twentieth century the Scottish Higher Leaving Certificate could not be awarded without Higher English (and the rest!). Not only did large numbers of Scots study Lyric Poetry – The Sonnet, but they learned sonnets by heart in anticipation of an oral examination by His (later, Her) Majesty's Inspectors of Schools. The oral was used to weed out the borderline candidates. Unsurprisingly, therefore, many of this writer's vintage can still reel off –

'When I consider how my light is spent,
'Ere half my days, in this dark world and wide,
And that one Talent which is death to hide,
Lodg'd with me useless...'

Like Beethoven and Milton, Geddes must have plumbed the depths of despair. For weeks he had to sit in a darkened room, with bandaged eyes. We know that Beethoven learned to adjust, giving up conducting and retiring into a private world where his inner ear helped him to create sublime music. Milton, eventually reconciled 'to only stand and wait', with the support of his women-folk conjured up one of the mightiest poems in the English language. For Geddes the experience of suffering was seminal.

'What can a visual, not auditive, do, if he be blind?' Condemned to sit in darkness, Geddes tried to use the experience positively, arranging his ideas and experiences into some sort of order. In the excellent television programme broadcast by BBC Scotland on 12 September 1970 – entitled *Eye for the Future – Patrick Geddes, 1854-1932* – there is a moving scene in which Leonard Maguire, a fine Scots character actor and the very image of Geddes, recreates Geddes' breakthrough. In a reconstruction – but not fictional – we see the bandaged Maguire/Geddes emerging from the house mumbling and thinking aloud. Behind him the door has nine panes of glass in its upper half and, in order to 'keep his place' Geddes feels for one pane and calls it something. He labels another, then another, then begins to think aloud about the relationships between one pane of glass and the next.

Geddes had discovered what he later called a 'thinking machine' and what we would call a 'mental map', not something driven by steam or thermionic valves, but a deceptively simple home-made device for clarifying thought and explaining relationships. All his life he was to use and develop them – often to the annoyance of colleagues. The *Notation of Life* (see Fig 10) was a thinking machine developed by Geddes many years later in India. The condensed notes amount to three-and-a-half pages and start – 'Take this double sheet of paper for our ledger of life...'

Fortunately for Geddes, the blindness passed away after some weeks. Although he had contrived to make an important personal advance during his illness it was obvious that long hours at the microscope were not for him. On his return to Britain there were difficult years ahead. Based in Edinburgh he held a number of posts on the fringe of the university, without success in achieving security. He got married and started a family. He travelled the country, lecturing more and more on sociological topics. More and more he became discontented as he realised that he wanted to teach but nobody wanted to employ him.

A measure of stability was achieved, however, when a patron endowed a personal, part-time, Chair of Botany for him at Dundee. At £200 per annum plus two-thirds of the students' fees it did not make him a wealthy man, but it gave a measure of security and structure for him and his growing family over the next thirty years. At £100 per annum he could employ an assistant to cover for him when necessary. Almost his first action was to lay out a small botanic garden in the grounds, complete with gardener. Much of the teaching took place there and would stray into the city, whose slums were eminently suitable for field study.

In the summer term the family usually lived in Newport, over the Tay from the city, but for most of this period they maintained a family home in Edinburgh. To describe this period of the Geddes's lives chronologically is beyond the skill of this writer, instead it is enough to state that it was a period of furious activity and sketch out some of the forms the activity took. It is important to note that these innovations did not follow each other in a neat sequence, they overlapped, they ran simultaneously, at times Geddes created for himself situations of such stress as would have crippled a lesser man. If Anna, his wife, sometimes seemed to their daughter and younger son wanting in 'over-flowing mother-love' this was probably the consequence of having to be the rock-like support of her husband and to run a household which could have turned into chaos over a weekend. After all, it was Lewis Mumford himself who said that tidying up after Geddes was like trying to put the contents of Vesuvius back into the crater after an eruption.

Over the centuries scores of writers have deplored the living conditions of the poor and trumpeted against their idleness and reluctance to help themselves. Geddes was special because, when he saw a problem he tried to do something about it and, as well as preaching, led by example. Six months after they were married, Anna and he moved into a flat in James Court, a near-slum off the Lawnmarket in the Royal Mile, and began improving it. Then they began to organise the neighbours into communal action, Geddes being seen in an old night-shirt painting the outside walls in light colours. Anna set up homemaking groups and a Saturday morning sewing club for the young girls.

PG was concerned that the Old Town had become a social sink when the New Town drained away the more prosperous folk. As the city grew in the late nineteenth century this process was accentuated as fine new suburbs spread out to the west and south. He tried to lure back people – often university types – who would help to recreate the medieval city where peers and prostitutes might share the same close. Ramsay Lodge built by the 18th century painter Allan Ramsay was remodelled and later a large block of flats added at right angles to form Ramsay Garden. In traditional style and freshly-painted and for the nine months of the year when its south side is not hidden by the scaffolding for the Edinburgh Military Tattoo, it is a magnificent sight, seen gleaming in the sun from miles around. In typical Geddesian fashion, it was recognised that people are different and the building contained flats of a mixture of sizes, unlike the bungalows of the 1930s suburbs or the endless modularity of more modern flats. Geddes's own flat was on the first floor, had eleven rooms and was sometimes beyond his means to keep.

Another series of ventures arose around student hostels. The Edinburgh tradition was for students to lodge in the town, in private homes. Geddes sought to encourage mixed communities and set up a series of student hostels in renovated properties around the Lawnmarket. Riddle's Court was a very old building where the Lord Provost of Edinburgh had entertained James VI and his new Queen, Anne of Denmark, three centuries previously. It had one of the painted ceilings common in Scotland around 1600. Geddes had a parallel ceiling painted in a large first-floor room. In true Geddes style it seeks to educate and inform the viewer about the development of Edinburgh University, especially the growth of democracy and what we now call student power. It is no coincidence that Riddle's Court was chosen for the ceiling, for it was the first self-governing hostel, certainly in Europe.

Geddes found it difficult to stand back, however, and we hear about his coming crashing in late at night and shouting – 'There's a glorious moon tonight, let's go and climb Arthur's Seat!' It would have taken a very strong mind to resist such an offer! Again, when there was some scandal about the behaviour of some of the young men and the housemaids, he found himself in a terrible quandary as one side of his brain reminded him that this was a self-governing community which should sort out the matter themselves and the other reminded him of his moral upbringing.

One of the traits that makes research into Geddes' activities so difficult is that, while he was a leader and a prophet and loved to stride ahead and show the way, he was also a genuine believer in self-help and participation and what we would now call empowerment. Thus he encouraged groups to survey, to plan and to manage wherever possible. In 1884 he set up the Environment Society to improve and renew the Old Town environment. It became the Edinburgh Social Union, an interesting title.

Geddes shared with Burns the wish to remake society. On the end of Ramsay Garden is a handsome sundial (Plate 7c) with two inscriptions, one in Greek and one in Scots – 'It's comin' yet for a' that'. No self-respecting Scot needs more, the poem – 'at once a prayer and a prophecy' – concludes:

'That Man to Man the warld o'er
Shall brithers be for a' that'.

At a time when everything possible was being done to increase agricultural output by eliminating the competition of weeds and pests, Burns wrote:

'To A Mouse
On Turning Her Up In Her Nest With The Plough
November 1785'

In it he expresses a tolerance for our fellow-creatures –

'I doubt na, whyles, but thou may thieve;
What then? Poor beastie, thou maun live!
A daimen icker in a thrave*
'S a sma' request;'   (*one ear of corn in 24 sheaves)

and tries to apologise on behalf of the human race,

'I'm truly sorry Man's dominion
Has broken Nature's social union,'

before emphasising the interdependence of all living creatures:-

'An' justifies that ill opinion
   Which makes thee startle
At me, thy poor, earth-born companion
   An' fellow-mortal.'

In changing their name from the Environment Society to the Edinburgh Social Union, they knew that they were making a statement of concern at the *status quo* and of intention to change it.

Any danger that Geddes might have turned into a narrow specialist botanist evaporated after the Mexico escapade and his temporary blindness, instead he had become a Big Botanist, advocating The Garden as a manifestation of the diversity of life, the beauty of flower and perfume, the change of the seasons, of the stewardship engendered by planting for succeeding generations, as a place where education through heart, hand and eye could be achieved. Even in the congested, built-up Old Town he and the ESU were able find dozens of scraps of unused space which they surveyed.

Plans were drawn up, the locals drawn in, seeds and plants obtained and all set to together to create little green islands amid the solid but darkly depressing masonry.

Short's Observatory was set up with telescopes and a camera obscura as a mid-Victorian semi-scientific tourist attraction. The 'Popular Observatory' had fallen on hard times when Geddes took it over in 1895, turned it into the Outlook Tower and set up what was described in 1899 as 'the world's first sociological laboratory'. Superbly situated on the tail of the Edinburgh Castle rock it is an old town-house converted into a five-storey tower-house. In the time of Geddes he led visitors to the very top at breakneck speed because he believed that this stimulated observation. From the top

Fig. 2 Site of Children's Garden, Johnston Terrace

The unprepossessing site hemmed in by walls and buildings. (Patrick Geddes Archive, University of Edinburgh).

Fig. 3 Castlehill School Garden,
Johnston Terrace

Neglect transformed. Neatly dressed pupils under supervision. Tree, lawn, flower
beds, vegetable plots and frame. (History of Education Centre Trust)

the view over south-east Scotland was observed and analysed. Down one
floor the camera obscura was used to focus on certain places and further observe
and analyse. Successive floors provided a concentric learning experience as one
moved down through Edinburgh to Scotland, to the English-speaking world,
Europe and the rest of the world.

The Outlook Tower became important in its own right, as a focus for
learning in and about the environment. It also became important as a centre
for Geddesian activities, as a symbol and as a model for similar developments
elsewhere by Geddes and others. The rooms were filled with three-dimen-
sional models and exhibitions and, as teaching and learning devices, these
were vigorously used by Geddes.

The task of designing the new zoological gardens on Corstorphine Hill
gave him the opportunity to display the power of his lateral thinking. Zoos
were essentially rows of heavily defended cages in front of which visitors
promenaded and gawped at the animals. Geddes started off with the concept
of a garden and created a space which was worth visiting without even seeing an
animal. Paths, walls and bridges covered the hillside, woodland and gardens

separated the animal houses and enclosures. Especially, Geddes turned upside-down the eighteenth century laird's view of his estate, looking out from the big house over the ha-ha to the animals grazing in the parks beyond. Using the old quarries he created large, open amphitheatres where the big cats could lounge in the sun or pace up and down with no obvious barrier between them and the visitor. (In fact, there was a big, hidden ditch and wall). The result was a seemingly natural setting for the animals. The writer remembers well an early visit to the Zoo and seeming to establish a rapport across to a polar bear, a big brown bear or a lion. The pleasure was heightened by the tension of wondering whether a lion could or could not leap across that gap, or a polar bear could jump out of the water and on to that wall.

Fig. 4 Part of the Edinburgh Room, Outlook Tower.

The windows look west to the Castle (right), south to the Pentlands (left), east and north (behind viewpoint)
(Patrick Geddes Archive, University of Edinburgh).

Patrick Geddes was a pioneer of summer schools. Using the student hostels during the summer holidays he started with two short courses in 'seaside Zoology and garden Botany'. Over the years the programme became longer, the range of topics wider and the teaching force more numerous, more influential and international. A photograph of one of his meetings in Ramsay Garden in the 1890s shows about fifty serious and responsible people ranged up and down the steps. About a third are youngish men in suits, wearing ties, mainly clean-shaven. There are a few older women, but most are youngish and dressed for summer. The straw hat was obviously the thing that year and all but a handful are wearing or carrying one. Clearly Geddes was satisfying a latent demand, particularly from young women, for serious education about major issues. There was energy seeking to be channelled into socially useful concerns, and he was the person to do it.

One Geddes commission leads into a consideration of the third way in which he operated in these pre-World War I years. Dunfermline is a medium-sized town in Fife. It was well-known for having been the capital in the reign of Malcolm Canmore, whose queen (later sanctified) regularly crossed to and from Edinburgh by the Queen's Ferry. The body of Robert the Bruce lay in its former abbey. Around 1903 it was a centre of world importance for the weaving of damask linen. In 1848 the Carnegie family emigrated to the United States where Andrew Carnegie prospered mightily, as the 'Star Spangled Scotchman' becoming one of the 'robber barons' dominating US society at the end of the nineteenth century.

Unlike most of the robber barons he had thoughts about wealth and a creed –

'...the man who dies leaving behind him millions of available wealth, which was free for him to administer during life... The man who dies thus rich dies disgraced.'

Selling out to the US Steel Corporation, he began, systematically, to give away his wealth – but with strings attached. Education was the way for the poor to fight their way out of poverty, so every town in Scotland willing to maintain it got a public library. No child should be prevented from going to school by poverty, so there were Carnegie boots and Carnegie schoolbags. Dunfermline, as his birthplace, received special treatment, and in 1903 Geddes was commissioned by the Carnegie Trust to prepare designs and proposals for the use of the Pittencrieff Estate (into which Carnegie had not been allowed to venture when a child and which he had now bought and was about to present to the citizens of Dunfermline in order to bring into 'the monotonous lives of the toiling masses of Dunfermline more of sweetness and light').

This was one of the first of many planning commissions undertaken by Geddes and he spared no energy or expense in surveying and preparing his report (he was eventually paid £750 in settlement of his bill for £798). Published as *City Development* his report was a masterpiece of its kind, being thorough, sweeping yet attentive to detail, innovatively illustrated and inspiring. Unfortunately, the Trustees got cold feet, and the Pittencrieff Park Dunfermline now has, while a perfectly decent lung for the good people of that town, represents a great opportunity missed.

Such commissions, surveys and reports were increasingly to become a major focus of Geddes's life and this kind of work took him all over Britain (Dublin was still in Britain at this date) and the world. Sofia Leonard has more to say on these activities at a later stage.

Most of our working activities contain elements of Development and Maintenance and our happiness and success may depend on our achieving the right balance between them. When the Forth Bridge opened in 1890 it was a staggering engineering development. That it was still in use at the end of the twentieth century without any of the original steelwork having had to be replaced was the result of continuous maintenance. Geddes was long on development but short on maintenance. He could think up ideas faster than anyone could ever implement and for him the thrill was in getting a project going. The Town and Gown Association often complained of his walking away, leaving them to hold the baby. Managers could be used, but almost by definition lacked the credal energy of the developer himself. Thus when the Outlook Tower had its first financial crisis, referred to earlier, Geddes's reaction was to try to increase his own teaching load, which might have benefitted a few more visitors but would certainly not have turned the business around.

As the new century moved on towards war, Geddes found himself more and more in distress. While he had considerable small-scale success and had a loyal following, his various enterprises gained him some celebrity but were not generating enough income. He still had to travel the country lecturing and had to take on work in Cyprus. Above all, he saw little sign of the world being changed in any significant way. The Edinburgh establishment was not recognising him adequately – although how could he expect support when he could write of them like this:

'Our Edinburgh legal idea of business which eliminates all consideration of feeling, individual or public, which attains the ideal and utmost coldness to all, coinciding with the lowest circle of the Inferno – that of Ice; for your own sake and that of others, why stay there?'

It took *A Letter From India* (see later) to point out that Gandhi and Geddes had the same birthday – although Geddes was fifteen years older. They had much in common and corresponded in cordial terms, but do not seem ever to have met. For Geddes, Gandhi was too much of the politician. Although Gandhi made much of his hand-spinning, Geddes found him deficient in understanding the value of forests and thus in basic understanding. It may be that, had Geddes been more like Gandhi, he might have achieved more.

Geddes was no politician, indeed he despised politicians. But Geddes was now finding out that, while it was immensely satisfying to be a prophet and denounce ignorance and prejudice, to be the boy who rings the doorbell and runs away, influential friends were hard to come by. It has to be said that his writing is dense and often obscure. Influenced by Carlyle, he somehow fails to use his tortured Germanic style to drive the message home, as the Sage of Chelsea could. His platform manner was not all that it might be. People who heard him could be uplifted or electrified, too often, however, 'not all of the lecturer's sentences cleared the bushy beard or got beyond the blackboard'.

He frequently showed a naivety touching in such a great and clever man. For example, at the end of the First World War he and a collaborating author published three books on *The Making of the Future*, analysing the ills of the world and putting forward solutions. Addressing the Allied nations who had just come through four years of terrible warfare, Geddes appeared to think that it was enough to point out the real causes of war and a logic for reconstruction for intelligent people to make a peace which would last. Whereas, as we know with hindsight, France used the Peace Conferences to exact revenge for the punitive peace of 1871, creating the conditions for the rise of a strong man who would, in turn, exact revenge for the punitive peace of 1919.

But there was always Alasdair. All Patrick and Anna's children were brought up in simple style at home, wherever that might be. At one stage they stayed just outside Dunfermline with an old friend who had looked after the children when they were very young and the parents were in Cyprus. 14 Ramsay Garden was let to improve the cash flow. The children received an education at home balancing 'heart, hand and heart', an 'education for peace'. For Alasdair the result was a young man of fine and steady character. He decided that he needed a year at Edinburgh Academy to make sure that he was not disadvantaged by the lack of conventional schooling – and did well there. He worked on farms and at the Millport Research Station. He went on an Arctic expedition. Although Patrick was very difficult to work with, father and son made a good team. However he felt underneath, Alasdair patiently carried out the maintenance function, ably supporting his father's many developments.

In the autumn of 1914, Alasdair (23) and father (sixtieth birthday on board ship) sailed for India. Alasdair fell in love with India but became restless with the opposing tensions of his father's work and events back in Europe. PG was a pacifist who had always been distressed by jingoism and Prussian militarism. His attitude towards violence is best summed up by his behaviour when in Mexico. Banditry was rife and Robert tried to convince his brother to carry a revolver when he rode out on field investigations. Patrick chose instead to carry the equivalent of £5 with him to buy off the bandits. If things turned violent he would use the kick-boxing he had recently learnt when in Paris. Perhaps fortunately, neither course of action had to be brought into play.

Geddes applied for leave of absence from Dundee in order that he might reorganise Belgium in summer 1915 – i.e. after the war! In the event, Alasdair and he were both back in Britain at that time. When Geddes set off again for India he took his wife, but not Alasdair. With admirable foresight he had learned to drive motor vehicles, then joined a course at the Roehampton School of Aeronautics and from there was commissioned into the Royal Naval Air Service.

For once the Army was able to find a square hole for this square peg. Instead of sending him at the head of his men, armed only with a pistol, over the top into uncut barbed wire and a hail of machine-gun bullets, they realised that his education and experience meant he could observe, analyse and record data, and communicate – so he was transferred to the Army Balloon Corps. Soon he was a field instructor and promoted to captain. In December 1916 he was awarded the MC for his reconnaissance work and made up to major. Liaison work with the French brought him the Cross of the Legion of Honour.

His sister Norah's husband, Frank Mears, served in his unit as captain and recorded a typical Geddesian incident. Bad weather had halted balloon operations so, to keep the men occupied, Alasdair borrowed a plough and horses and taught his men how to plough the devastated fields around them. He had at least one narrow escape in the air but it was while walking back to his unit from an observation post between the lines that he was struck by a shell fragment and killed instantly.

Geddes was so devastated that he could not bring himself to break the news to Anna, who was with him in India. Having been informed of his son's death by telegram there was a period of several weeks when letters from Alasdair continued to arrive in India by mail steamer. Anna was in hospital in Lucknow and in a doctor friend's house in Calcutta and Geddes would read her Alasdair's letters as they arrived. When running a summer school in Darjeeling he was summoned to Calcutta to find that Anna had just died.

Patrick and Anna had been loving partners, perhaps too close for the entire good of their children, as well as a formidable pair of 'do-gooders'. The effect of the double calamity on his life was to leave him in a more disorganised state than ever. He still had ideas, he still had energy, but some of the sparkle had gone and a frantic note often creeps in. Lewis Mumford told the pathetic tale of their first meeting, in New York:

'...he took me squarely by the shoulders and gazed at me intently 'You are the image of my poor dead lad,' he said to me with tears welling in his eyes, 'and almost the same age he was when he was killed in France. You must be another son to me Lewis, and we will get on with our work together.' There was both grief and desperation in this appeal: both too violent, too urgent for me to handle.'

Mumford and Alasdair differed in almost every respect, in appearance, in training, in character and Mumford had no intention of becoming anyone's surrogate. Yet there were moments when Mumford found his life shaken to the core by Geddes, who

'conveyed what it is like to be fully alive, alive in every pore, at every moment, in every dimension.'

Norah was much less tolerant of her father's excesses than Alasdair, often being torn between trying to satisfy PG's expectations of her and following her own path. The most determined of the three children, she ran the Outlook Tower in her father's absence before deciding to become a landscape gardener; like Alasdair in working with her father to carry out his projects. In 1915 she married Frank Mears (later Sir Frank Mears) who had been secretary of the Outlook Tower and Geddes's co-worker, for example, in preparing the Edinburgh Room at the first British Town Planning Conference, sponsored by the Royal Institute of British Architects. Mears and Geddes worked well together but Mears managed to avoid being swallowed up, establishing a practice which has adapted and survived until the present.

Arthur (born 1895) was 'a much more delicate and nervous child than Alasdair'. Patrick and Anna loved their children and thought deeply about how best to bring them up but may have been too busy or too harassed to do this with any warmth. For the winter terms of 1906 and 1907 Arthur was miserable in a Board school with sixty in a class. In 1908 he attended Dundee High School. Continuity and consistency are supposed to be essential for good schooling: is it any surprise that Arthur at this time was said to be a 'brilliant and promising child – with nerves?' Arthur's imaginative and nervous temperament needed time to be understood and time was at a premium *chez* Geddes.

The anecdote which follows says a great deal about Arthur. In 1910 Geddes and the two boys went to Dundee for the summer term. Alasdair was to be his father's assistant while Arthur was to continue his education of 'head, heart and hand' by being tutored in woodcarving and other subjects. In 2004 one can stand at the entrance to Wardrop's Court, in the Lawnmarket, and see two fine gilded dragons in the archway leading to one of the former student hostels. (In Geddesland, where we now are, we must remember that a dragon is not just a dragon. It is a symbol of sin and of evil, hence George and the Dragon. In the Celtic lands it has an association with chieftainship and power). Inside the entrance is another pair of dragons, but one is rather rough and definitely crude. Poor Arthur, that he should turn out to be not very good with his hands. Yet he had done the work and that deserved recognition, so there is Arthur's dragon still (Plate 7b).

Arthur was eighteen at the outbreak of war in 1914 'and not nearly as strong and confident as Alasdair'. A pacifist, he still felt he had to do something. He worked on a farm, presumably so that someone else could join up. He volunteered for the Army Field Ambulance Unit, but was turned down on health grounds. He found a place in the Society of Friends War Victims Relief organisation so that he, too, served in France, but under a different banner. Arthur was expected to take over from Alasdair and went with his father to India and Montpellier after the war, where he learned, as Alasdair had learnt before him, that 'no human being could live as well as work with PG and survive'. Arthur ended his professional career in the Geography department of Edinburgh University where the writer's life was touched by that of Arthur Geddes tangentially at five or six points. He was brilliant and inspiring at some times, at others he could be irritating and frustrating – but the writer may not have been ready enough in his acceptance. Kenneth Maclean has more to say on his influence on Geographical Education in a later essay.

For Patrick Geddes the First World War caused damage at the personal level. Intellectually, he was in despair at the insanity of nations. What might, for a lesser man, have been the last straw, came as a result of enemy action. The Edinburgh Room of the RTPI exhibition of 1910 was expanded into a Cities Exhibition – the first of its kind anywhere – and toured, to great acclaim, such cities as Edinburgh, Dublin, Belfast and Paris (although it lost money on the way). When Alasdair and Patrick sailed off to India in the SS *Nore* the exhibition was packed into the *Clan Grant* for them to use in India. They arrived safely at Bombay in mid-October. On the 23rd the *Clan Grant*, and with it the Cities Exhibition, was sent to the bottom of the sea by the German commerce raider *Emden*. Years of work were lost in a few moments – and with them another chance to turn over some cash.

Geddes, however, bounced back. Friends and colleagues rallied round, the Outlook Tower was used and a replacement exhibition put together. Geddes was offered a specially-created Chair of Sociology and Civics at Bombay University and the exhibition found a permanent base there, going out on tour when appropriate. Compensation for the loss of the original exhibition was promised and ultimately arrived – £2,054 – in 1926. In 1925 a Civil List pension of £80 was awarded. Geddes was now over seventy and the establishment felt safe to recognise him at last. In 1912 a Knighthood for PG had been there for the taking, but was declined 'on democratic grounds'. When offered again, under Ramsay Macdonald's government in 1931, he accepted 'on business grounds', hoping that the award would give him powers of persuasion previously denied to him! He was not to enjoy the benefits of the award for long. The investiture for the so-called New Year's Honours List had to be delayed till February because of the illness of George V, and Geddes had to linger in London's 'hellish atmosphere' until he developed breathing problems. Returning to Montpellier, he died on 17 April 1932 and was cremated in Marseilles.

Most of Geddes's life after 1914 was spent abroad. Sofia Leonard deals with that in the next chapter, so that all that is necessary here is the briefest of summaries. Late in 1918, while the war was still in progress but Palestine had just been freed by the British, Geddes was invited by the Zionist Commission to plan a new university for Jerusalem and to advise on its wider problems. The planning was comparatively easy, politics and implementation were quite another story. His words of 1919 resonate eerily in our time:

'The fears of unending strife between Jew, Arab and Christian over Palestine do not exist for me. There is never any permanent need for people to kill each other'.

Geddes (and Arthur) travelled to many parts of the Indian subcontinent surveying cities and drawing up plans for their improvement. Sofia in more detail examines the same problem of following excellent planning ideas with decisive action – what we might call 'the Dunfermline problem'.

His retirement at sixty-five from his Dundee chair meant a drop in income but set him free from its chains, however lightly worn. In 1924, Geddes wrote:

'This adventure is prospering, and my old cottage is growing on each side and back, and quite as a small chateau with its Outlook Tower on quarry cliffs and future rock garden below... has got for me the place I told you of, at Domme in Dordogne – the windmill and site – for under £100, and yesterday I bought at auction a cottage of 4 rooms near this, in good condition, with ample annexes etc., and cistern and well, with 7/8 acre of meadow, for – exactly £50...

I am offered an intermediate house, on next hillside from this... with some 7-8 acres of good land for £400, and wish I had it handy'.

What are we, having read so often *How I took an Old Mill in Provence and converted it into a Bijou Residence despite the Picturesque but Rascally Natives* or watched a host of programmes about the perils of buying property abroad, to make of this behaviour? Had Geddes succumbed to the *maladie des pierres* which affects citizens of the sun-starved north bedazzled by *la lumière éblouissante* of Alphonse Daudet's Provence? Geddes had always dreamed of extending his Summer Schools to an international college and here he was, in his seventies, proposing to set up Le Collège des Écossais just outside Montpellier.

When most men of his age would have been rewriting history in their memoirs, Geddes was once again working (HAND, Heart and Head) to turn his ideas into solid form. The upper terrace garden was laid out as a botanical thinking-machine (the Royal Botanic Garden in Edinburgh has a whole row of these now). From its own Outlook Tower the Valley Section could be observed and analysed.

The Scots College polarised emotions. Norah complained about 'Thinking machines for breakfast, dinner and supper'. Arthur was blackmailed into staying there while he studied for three years at the ancient university of Montpellier and completed his doctoral thesis. Those who thought to use the college as a 'crammers' to brush up their French and Mathematics took little from their time there.

The words of another ex-student, quoted below, paraphrase the reminiscences of others, perhaps already more mature:

'Despite the fact that my chances of a successful Oxford career were not materially advanced during my stay in Montpellier, I could not have had a happier, a more interesting and enjoyable time. I do not regret a moment of it.

I readily acquired a cosmopolitan attitude of mind. I liked all my fellow collegiates enormously. We were together most of the time when we were not engaged in our own work. There was an exceptionally harmonious and light-hearted atmosphere about the College des Ecossais.

... But it was Geddes himself, although he moved among us vaguely and almost aimlessly and though he never interfered in or cared about what we were doing, who set the real mark on the College des Ecossais and made our stay there so memorable'.

Superficially it might look as though the last few years of Geddes's life were a period of decline. Formally retired from the discipline, however light, of his university posts it could be said – and was – that he was thrashing around irresponsibly. Yet others saw a different Geddes, free from the discipline of the contract, although not, regrettably, from the grind of having to raise money to finance his ploys of old age.

On being told not to overwork he wrote to his daughter, Norah:

'While it is very kind of all one's friends to want to take care of the old man, it's no use for 'Old-and-Bold' ... I'm still out for adventure, for all risks; and did not need Nietzsche to teach me to live dangerously!'

To her he described his life in India:

'So, with hard work – motoring, with constant descents and plannings on foot – active talking, explaining, arguing, and winning decisions; and then at the planning table at every available moment, I am ready for sleep, which always comes. Truly work is the best anodyne!'

To Lilian Brown, later his second wife, he is the happy warrior describing the early days at the Scots College:

'Here now these seven weeks, hard at work building and gardening, and with constant supervision of both; half a dozen gardeners at it – not to speak of masons, joiners, tilers etc. I've not had such a time since making Dundee garden, and building Ramsay Garden – for though this is a much smaller affair, it is more complex.'

He goes on:

'So you see I'm greatly pleased with place, and with myself, as again happily at real work – open air all day long – and bed after bread and milk supper – say 8 pm – to begin next day with a spate of thinking, from 5. 4. 3. (or 2.) am as the case may be, and before going up to work, at 7 or 7.30 or 8. I am only writing today – and the first non-business letter for long – because it is pouring, and no-one can work!'

The Indian lawyer, Pheroze R Barucha, once a student at the Scots College, made this comment on the swift denouement of PG's life:

'He achieved the death he deserved – that of the good worker and the good fighter. When the hour struck he went, without having the time for suffering, unseemly struggle or regret'.

Finding Geddes Abroad

Sofia Leonard

PATRICK GEDDES IS BETTER known abroad than in Edinburgh. I have done a good deal of travelling in my lifetime and wherever I have gone, I can fairly say with Patrick Abercrombie that 'I found Geddes coming back'!

I heard about Patrick Geddes for the first time when I studied at the Planning Institute of Lima, Peru in 1963. This was an international school of planning for South American postgraduates, the first of its kind. Though linked to Yale University, its lecturers were mainly from Peru and Argentina, and had mostly been trained in Paris. This is why our course in Lima was largely based on Le Play, Demolins and, of course, Patrick Geddes.

Geddes's book *Cities in Evolution* had just then been published in a Spanish translation by Jorge Hardoy, the well-known architect-planner from Argentina and colleague of Percy Johnson-Marshall, of whom more later. The book immediately became required reading for planning students in Latin America, making Patrick Geddes a familiar name among architects and planners in the continent. So it was in Lima that I learned about the 'Valley Section' and its uses in Regional Planning, and our school planning projects addressed human settlements in river valleys in Peru in a direct application of Geddes's principles.

At that distance in time and place, Geddes was known as a remarkable 'English' professor who had worked for many years in India and whose work had great significance for developing countries. It was some years later, when I came to live in Edinburgh after my marriage, that I found Patrick Geddes to be in fact Scottish, and that an important part of his life's work had been dedicated to the regeneration of the Old Town in Edinburgh. But I found too, to my surprise, that Geddes was at that time largely unknown in Scotland except for a small number of admirers in University circles. But that was later on; as a young student in Lima I could not envisage then that one day I would come to Edinburgh and work with the Geddes Collection at the Outlook Tower.

Travel is my theme here. I want here to touch on Patrick Geddes's travels, both literal and intellectual, with occasional asides where in my own life I have, so to speak, brushed against Geddes in different parts of the world. Travel was not incidental but rather integral to Geddes's career and to the development of his thought – and action. His ideas, though naturally grounded in the Scottish cultural tradition, gained enormously from his extensive journeys and contacts with America, Europe and the Indian Sub-continent.

America

After Lima, for the second year of my post graduate studies, I transferred to Yale, full of anticipation at joining one of America's great 'Ivy League' Universities. The Yale City Planning department was then a wonderful place for a student in her twenties! New England is a region where nature is at its best in autumn and special in spring. It was at Yale that I met my husband, a fact that changed the course of my life and gave me the chance to come to live in Edinburgh.

I found much of which Geddes would have approved at Yale. The City Planning programme was not part of an isolated and sterile campus but, like the rest of the University, and like Edinburgh, it lay in the very heart of its city – New Haven in Connecticut, some 75 miles from New York. Rather less in the Geddesian spirit, the University, even in the mid-1960s, accepted only men as undergraduates, but fortunately for me this restriction did not apply to the postgraduate schools.

The programme shared the magnificent building, in 1964 quite new, designed by Paul Rudolf to house the departments of Art, Architecture and City Planning. It was indeed an inspirational environment. Equivalent to about eight storeys high, and with a splendid penthouse for parties and other events, it had some 27 internal levels. At its centre was a hollow space, about 30 metres high. Here the floor was used for open 'crits' and on a high pedestal there was a life size reproduction of the goddess Athena from the Parthenon, presiding over the architecture and planning studios disposed all around in balcony-like spaces. Surely Geddes would have smiled. It was immensely stimulating to work cheek by jowl with Serge Chermayeff and Paul Rudolf's architecture students, and with talented painters and sculptors then immersed in the thrills of the new Op-pop movement. The 'buzz' was great!

Yet if the spirit of Geddes seemed present all around me – in space and in dynamism of interaction – the difference in academic approach could hardly have been more striking. Geddes was not given the same importance at Yale as in Lima: his ideas and methods did not form the core of the Planning programme. This was a great disappointment for me. But it was compensated, at least in part, insofar as Lewis Mumford was required reading in Christopher Tunnard's History of Planning course. Herein lay another link with Geddes. It was through Tunnard's splendid lectures that I learned more about Lewis Mumford, Geddes's most prominent American disciple.

Patrick Geddes had travelled to America several times before meeting Mumford quite late in his career. His first trip was in the autumn of 1898 when he visited New York and Philadelphia. He stayed for three months, lecturing and trying to find sponsors for his project of the moment, the International Summer Meeting at the Paris *Exposition Universelle*. Geddes was organising in this connection an International Association for the Advancement of Science and Art and he was trying to gather support on both sides of the Atlantic for construction of Paul Reclus's gigantic globe, intended for the Paris exhibition and estimated to cost £200,000, an enormous sum for that time.

Geddes found New York:

'startling beyond anything I had expected ...fearfully and wonderfully made, sublime and ridiculous in one ... The flying cars, the ubiquitous overhead railways making the streets sordid skeleton tunnels, are extraordinarily efficient. There is no comparison between New York and London in this respect; the former is the place to move about in – but the latter for quiet life!'

Thanks to a letter of introduction from Professor Gréard, president of the University of Paris, Geddes, on his second trip in 1899, made contact with the most renowned of the American universities, Yale, Princeton, John Hopkins, Columbia and Harvard. His first of a programme of four lectures at Harvard addressed the 'Evolution of Sex'. Apparently, six hundred Bostonians turned out attracted by the title. Numbers dwindled for subsequent lectures, perhaps through disappointed curiosity or maybe because, as was often the case, his long sentences and Scottish accent could not quite negotiate past his bushy beard!

Patrick Geddes was already in his old age and a widower when he met Lewis Mumford, then only twenty seven years old. Mumford had read Geddes's Dunfermline report and had become interested in his work. He wrote to the Outlook Tower in 1916 to enquire about any courses running there, but Geddes was *en route* for India and they started to correspond instead. By 1919 Geddes was considering Mumford as a future collaborator and potentially his intellectual heir. Mumford agreed to organise a special course of lectures for Geddes at the New School for Social Research in New York. But the meeting between master and disciple did not go as expected. Geddes was eager to find someone 'to transform the accumulated seekings and findings of a lifetime into an orderly, readable form' and he thought that the young American would fit the bill. But Mumford, overwhelmed by Geddes's emotional demands and expectations, was put off this task as he explained in his 1966 essay, 'The Disciple's Rebellion'.

Geddes and Mumford differed in personality as much as in age. Geddes was a doer, a man of action, whereas Mumford was an intellectual. They simply did not 'click'. It did not help either that at the end of the visit, in Mumford's words,

'... he left me to the dreary task of packing his bags and papers – those heaps of clothes, those middens of notes and charts, those shelves of new books!... it was like putting the contents of Vesuvius back into the crater after an eruption!'

How I sympathised with Mumford when many years later it was my task, as curator of the University of Edinburgh's Patrick Geddes Collection at the Outlook Tower, to make sense of the accumulated records of Geddes's life work!

Possibly the most important example of Patrick Geddes's influence in action in North America was the Tennessee Valley Authority (TVA). In 1933, one year after the death of Geddes, the American Congress voted to establish a decentralised governmental agency to reconstruct an entire region for the benefit of all the inhabitants in this huge river valley. Political action by the Roosevelt administration can be traced to the 'Valley Section' of Patrick Geddes through David Lilienthal, first director of the TVA, Benton Mackaye and Lewis Mumford.

Europe

I came to live in Edinburgh in the Autumn of 1969. The cultural shock on arrival was almost as great as the climatic shock. I found the darkness of my first winter almost unbearable and very depressing. However, it was in Edinburgh that I re-found my connection with Geddes. My husband had studied at the Department of Architecture created by Sir Robert Matthew. Soon after arrival, I met Professor Percy Johnson-Marshall and his wife April who gave me a wonderful welcome and an introduction to the planning and architectural academic world in Edinburgh. Percy had studied in Liverpool under Sir Patrick Abercrombie and I soon learned that the attics of the Planning Department contained Geddes's famous 'Cities Exhibition' and other important papers pertaining to Geddes. The collection was in storage awaiting the refurbishment of the Outlook Tower, which had recently been purchased by the University to house the Patrick Geddes Centre for Planning Studies. This was a pet project of Percy's that did not materialise until his retirement in 1985.

Patrick Geddes, though naturally grounded in the Scottish cultural tradition, gained much from his extensive travels and contacts with Europe. European currents of thought had strong influence on Geddes's ideas and thinking.

When the young Patrick had gone to Roscoff, in Brittany, to recuperate from a bout of bad health, he struck up a friendship with Henri de Lacaze-Duthiers (1821-1901), a fellow biologist. This friendship was to start a close association with French colleagues which Geddes was to maintain throughout his lifetime. Paris was to become Geddes's spiritual home and it was here that Geddes learned about the sociologist Frederic Le Play (1802-1886). His young contemporary, Edmond Demolins (1852-1907), also a sociologist, was a follower of Le Play and introduced him to Le Play's famous triad, 'Place-Work-Folk': 'Place', the force of the environment which everywhere influenced what sort of work people do; 'Work', the conditioning factor of family type and organisation; and 'Folk', the fundamental social unit.

Le Play was also the first to combine personal field observation with statistical survey methods. A mining engineer by profession, he had travelled extensively throughout Europe making first hand studies of workers' groups. His aim was to gather concrete and comparative information on wages, family budgets, housing and stability of employment. Geddes gained from him the conviction that the functioning of society could be systematically studied, tested and eventually modified.

Demolins introduced Geddes too to the visual image of a valley with the symbols of different occupations. To this idea and image, Geddes added later his own diagram of the valley in profile and in birds' eye view – the celebrated 'Valley Section'. Its purpose was to show, visually, the hierarchy of settlements in a region where the primary occupations in the countryside were complemented by the secondary and tertiary occupations of the city's inhabitants, thus making the close link between the city and the region the basis of 'bio-regionalism'.

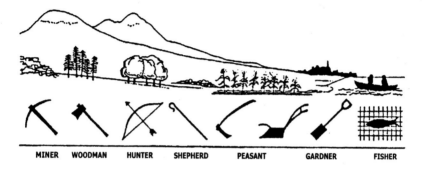

Fig. 5 The Valley Section in its simplest form
(Bulletin of Environmental Education)

In France too Geddes came to know and to study the work of Auguste Comte (1798-1857), philosopher, sociologist and founder of Positivism, born in Montpellier, a place that would attract Geddes particular interest late in life. In Comte's lectures on positivist philosophy all sciences were regarded as having passed from earlier theological and then metaphysical stages into a new positive or experiential stage. In positive ideology, the object of reverence was humanity and the core aim was to achieve the well-being and progress of human kind. Geddes, influenced by Comte, was later to advocate, and practise, an approach to the study of cities based on empirical research and inductive reasoning, directed towards social improvement and the 'Ascent of Man'.

Geddes attended regularly the British and French Association meetings held at Dover and Boulogne between 1870 and 1880. These international Association meetings on both sides of the Channel were a forum for examining new ideas in Sociology and Geography. His European contacts and interest widened further after his marriage to Anna Morton in 1886. Anna had been educated in Germany and had many contacts there.

At Jena in Germany Geddes gained much from contact with Ernst Heinrich Häckel (1834-1919). A naturalist born in Potsdam, Häckel had studied at Würzburg and Vienna and was now professor of zoology at Jena (1862-1909). At Geddes's invitation he participated as lecturer in several of Geddes's Summer Meetings in Edinburgh. Häckel was a strong supporter of Charles Darwin's

(1809-82) theories of evolution and his book *Ökologie* published in 1869, about the interaction between Organism and Environment, was to be highly influential in Geddes's work. At Jena, too, Geddes was much impressed by a 'comparative-type' or 'index' of species and it was this that led him to the idea of the Outlook Tower in Edinburgh in 1892.

The Outlook Tower, described as 'Geddes's thinking in three dimensions', was to be a type-Museum of the Universe, the synthesis of Art and Science – a place where Geddes intended to change the attitudes of ordinary Edinburgh citizens and open their minds to a wider evolutionary outlook.

Geddes's 'zoological meetings' at Granton in Edinburgh in 1886 were initially fairly local in character, perhaps inspired by similar meetings he had attended in Chautaugua, New York, although he developed his courses along different lines. They later developed into the celebrated Edinburgh Summer Meetings. Under the motto *Vivendo Discimus*, these became a regular feature of his activities at the Outlook Tower and they further strengthened Geddes's European links. One of the many European figures invited to the Summer Schools was Henri Louis Bergson (1859-1941).

Born in Paris, a philosopher and highly original thinker, Bergson became something of a cult figure in Europe, associated with the idea of the *Élan Vital* or 'creative impulse'. For Bergson, the *élan vital*, rather than Darwin's deterministic natural selection, was at the heart of evolution. For him intuition, rather than analysis, reveals the real world of process and change. Geddes shared with Bergson his belief in intuition and creative impulse. He often encouraged his students at the Summer Meetings to have pencil and paper always with them even by their bedside to write down an idea or inspiration at any time of the day or night.

Geddes went on to create his own Summer Meeting with international speakers in English, French, German and Russian, at the *Exposition Universelle* in Paris in 1900. Even more than at the Edinburgh Summer Meetings, this international school presented a full challenge to his intellectual and linguistic abilities. In Paris, there were the other attractions of the *Exposition*, its world-wide exhibits and scientific congresses. Geddes set out to use the 1900 *Exposition* as a vast laboratory to test his sociological ideas and his system for unifying knowledge.

In this Patrick was greatly helped, as always, by his wife Anna. Indispensable to him as wife, general manager and diplomat, Anna was a pillar of support to all his activities. In spite of suffering a late miscarriage at the time, she kept track of his appointments and applied tact and social grace when feathers were ruffled. Even their elder children, Norah and Alasdair, then 12 and 9 years old, were roped in to help with the great amount of clerical work involved.

Incidentally, it was at the *Exposition Universelle* that John Duncan's well-known set of educational stained-glass panels expressing Geddes's ideas, including the 'Valley Section', the *Arbor Seculorum* and the *Lapis Philosophorum* or Obelisk, were exhibited for the first time. Geddes himself brought the panels back to Edinburgh for the Outlook Tower. Murdo Macdonald's contribution on 'Patrick Geddes: Environment and Culture' examines the Valley Section panel in some detail. After the Exposition, John Duncan departed to take up a post at the new Chicago Arts Institute.

In 1913, the first 'World Congress of Cities' took place within the great Exposition Internationale at Ghent, the 'Flemish capital', and Geddes was awarded the Grand Prix for his 'Cities and Town Planning' Exhibition. The Congress had come into being through the efforts of his friend Paul Otlet, creator of the Mundaneum (World Centre for the Organisation of Knowledge) in Brussels, and of senator Henri La Fontaine who was awarded the Nobel Peace Prize later that year.

As a student, Patrick Geddes had been greatly inspired by Charles Darwin and his evolutionist theories. However, later on, he rejected those who used Darwinism to justify competitive trade or open warfare. He advocated instead the Russian prince Pyotr Alexeyevich Kropotkin's (1842-1921) 'mutual aid and co-operation'. Kropotkin, Moscow-born geographer and revolutionary, received his education in St Petersburg. In 1871 he renounced his title and became an anarchist. His was a peaceful anarchism centred on mutual support and trust in a harmonious society without government and hierarchies, very different from the lawlessness and chaos often associated with the idea.

Another anarchist, Elisée Reclus (1830-1905), one of seven remarkable brothers and a refugee after the Paris Commune, was a geographer and author of the vast Géographie Universelle (1894). Patrick Geddes invited Reclus to work with him at the Outlook Tower in Edinburgh. Their intellectual collaboration was later consolidated by family ties: Geddes's son Arthur married Jeannie Colin, daughter of old family friends in Montpellier and niece of Reclus. Geddes benefitted not only from Reclus's huge knowledge and understanding of the Earth, but also his sensitivity to the small scale. Reclus's book for children, L'Histoire d'un Ruisseau, in which a brook descending from its source in the mountains meets different types of people in various occupations, was a further inspiration to consolidate Geddes's regional concept of the Valley Section linking geography with sociology and anthropology.

It was the anarchists who inspired Geddes with the idea that regeneration in a depressed area is achieved through action by the people themselves through mutual aid and collaboration rather than competition – in today's words through 'empowerment of communities'. The key was to empower residents to achieve a better environment for themselves rather than waiting for action by government or charitable agencies. Geddes put this idea to the test brilliantly in his regeneration of the Old Town of Edinburgh (1890-1914).

I attended a seminar of the International Society of City and Regional Planners in Monte Verità in April 1997. As always, ISOCARP had selected the location brilliantly and I enjoyed the company of friends and colleagues amidst one of Europe's most beautiful landscapes. The seminar gave me the opportunity to learn something of the remarkable community of artists, thinkers, anarchists and theosophists who had greatly influenced Geddes.

The community flourished at the turn of the century at Monte Verità, a small pyramid-shaped mountain above Lake Maggiore close by Ascona, near Locarno. Monte Verità has been a special place since pre-historic times, having been a centre for pagan worship and it seems since then to have been a special source of inspiration: one of its more recent associations is with the modernist dancer and choreographer, Isadora Duncan.

A leading member of the Monte Verità community was the Moscow-born Mikhail Aleksandrovich Bakunin (1814-1876) who had taken part in the German revolutionary movement in 1848-9. He provides one link to Geddes in that Reclus was a member of his 'confraternity for anti-authoritarian socialism'. There is now an exhibition in one of the buildings in the complex at Monte Verità covering Bakunin's time there. Another prominent member of the confraternity was Yelena Petrovna Blavatsky (1831-1891), described as the most important occultist of the 19th century. Blavatsky, born in Yekaterinoslav in the Ukraine, went to America in 1873. Two years later she founded the Theosophical Society in New York and was later to carry her work to India. Another link to Geddes is through a close collaborator of Blavatsky, Annie Besant (1857-1933), a Londoner. Geddes had personally tutored her in Biology in the evenings when he was a student at the School of Mines in London – this at a time when women were still denied access to a University education. We will find Annie Besant again in India, this time helping Geddes to meet prominent figures in Indian culture.

One of the last activities of Patrick Geddes's life was the creation of the Scots College, or *Collège des Écossais*, complete with Outlook Tower, at Montpellier in 1924. He may have chosen the city for a number of reasons, not the least being family connection and the attraction of a good climate for his failing health. It was to the College that he invited Charles Flahault (1852-1935), his old friend and celebrated botanist, to lecture. International guests, and some students, started arriving. They included the American Philip Boardman, Geddes's biographer. I met Boardman in Edinburgh when he was 94 years of age. The occasion was the First Lecture of the Patrick Geddes Centre for Planning Studies, described by the late Kitty Michaelson of Edinburgh College of Art as 'a truly Geddesian event'. The speakers were Boardman, André Schimmerling, president of the *Association Patrick Geddes* in Montpellier and Helen Meller of Nottingham University.

Patrick Geddes died in Montpellier, in 1932.

India

Lord Pentland, then Secretary of State for Scotland, had seen Patrick Geddes's 'Cities Exhibition' when it was shown to great acclaim at the Royal Scottish Academy in Edinburgh in 1911. He had made the opening speech and became a great admirer and patron of Geddes. When he was appointed Governor of the Madras Presidency, Pentland asked Geddes to take the Cities Exhibition to tour in India. The overall aim for this visit was to develop the study and practice of city survey in India and to advise the British Administration on the vast problems of social and civic improvement, then becoming all too apparent. In the event Geddes was to work in India for nine years on and off. After the initial study of thirteen towns in the Madras Presidency, he completed a further 47 surveys in British India.

The Cities Exhibition was packed and shipped in the SS *Clan Grant* for the voyage to India on the eve of the Great War. Patrick and Alasdair took a different passage and this was fortunate as the *Clan Grant* was attacked and sunk by the destroyer *Emden* in the Indian Ocean. The loss of the Exhibition was a tragedy for Geddes, but amazingly the whole was replaced in only two months. Geddes's friends and colleagues had rallied around in an 'emergency committee' chaired by Dr HV Lanchester and including Frank Mears, Capper (architect for Ramsay Garden), Aitken and others. Their replacement Cities Exhibition followed largely the catalogue of the original exhibition at the RIBA Town Planning Exhibition at the Royal Academy in 1910. Shipped without further hitch, it toured India, being finally installed at the University of Bombay, where Geddes was appointed Professor of Civics and Sociology. Geddes worked in Bombay from 1919 until 1923 when his health broke down and he 'retired' to Montpellier in the south of France.

Geddes had the talent and good fortune to have friends not only in high places, but also among the growing Indian independence movement, and among philosophers, thinkers and artists. Here he was helped by Annie Besant whom we have seen before and who kept contact with Geddes throughout her life. In India, she introduced Geddes to Mohandas Karamchand Gandhi (1869-1948).

Venerated in his own lifetime as a moral teacher with the title of *Mahatma* (great soul), Gandhi was a reformer who sought an India not only independent but also free from caste and materialism. He was a great influence for peace not only for India but for the world. Geddes too was also a passionate advocate for peace, a belief further consolidated after the death of his son, Alasdair, in action in World War I, and peace was a theme frequently pursued in his lectures. Boardman hails him as 'peace-warrior'.

Annie Besant also introduced Geddes to Jiddu Krishnamurti (1895-1986) a Theosophist born in Madras and educated in England. He was taken up by Annie Besant who proclaimed him an incarnation of the Buddha, or 'Universal

Master'. He advocated a way of life and thought free from the narrowness of nationality, race and religion. In Calcutta, Patrick enjoyed close collaboration with the poet and philosopher Rabindranath Tagore (1861-1941). He worked with Tagore, at Santiniketan, for the creation of a University which would blend Eastern and Western philosophical and educational systems and would bring about an enlightened education for the future.

The idea of a 'university for the future' was very appealing to Geddes who was always arguing, in his own Scottish universities, for reform that would break the divides between the different faculties and would promote a multi-disciplinary education for all. He tried too to put these ideas into practice in 1919-20 with the University of Jerusalem, with only very partial success.

Geddes made three visits to India. He made the first (1914-1915) with his eldest son Alasdair. On his second visit (1915-1917) he was accompanied by his wife Anna Morton who, alas, and as we shall see, was never to return to Edinburgh. On his third trip (1919-1922) he was accompanied by his younger son Arthur.

I have tried to follow in Geddes footsteps in India, but this is no easy

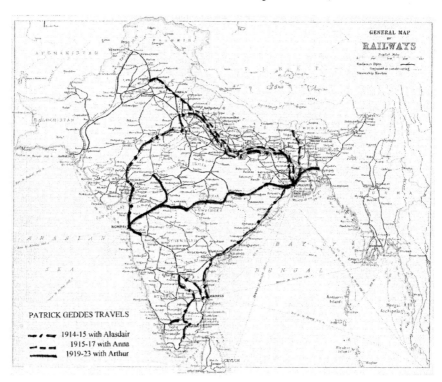

Fig. 6 The Travels of Geddes in India, 1914-15, 1915-17, 1919-23.
(*Imperial Gazetteer Atlas of India, 1909*)

undertaking. India is rightfully called a subcontinent. Distances are enormous, regions are very diverse and there are different peoples speaking many different languages. How did Geddes manage on his first trip to go from Bombay to Delhi, Agra, Jaipur and Calcutta in the north covering some hundreds of miles, and then turn south in order to meet up with Lord Pentland in Madras on the Bay of Bengal? Even more, how did he manage to fit in so many city surveys as well?

In four separate trips I have been able to cover only a miniscule part of Geddes's itinerary. On my first visit, I went to Delhi, Agra, Jaipur, Benares and Bombay. It was my first, and almost overpowering, taste of India. The mixture of sounds, colours, smells and the heat and humidity attack all your senses at once; it needs a while to get adjusted and take things in. I had been invited to give a talk about Patrick Geddes at the Delhi Institute. The building has a number of lecture rooms and when I arrived clutching my notes and my box of slides, I found that, at the same time – and in the room next door to mine, the Dalai Lama was to give a lecture! I was fretting that, perhaps, everyone would flock to hear the Dalai Lama and I would be talking to an empty room. I would have liked to go there myself! In the event I needn't have worried. Delhi proved that the name of Patrick Geddes was not forgotten. Soon my room was filled to the rafters with students and professional planners eager to hear about the 'Father of Town Planning'.

I found out that in India cities grow sequentially in spatial terms. When an area becomes derelict, or too run down or polluted, the town simply moves on to a new site nearby and the old place is abandoned. There are at least eleven different Delhis from different historic periods – side by side and not on top of each other as in most European cities. Each period has its own physical characteristics and landmarks including of course Sir Edwin Lutyen's New Delhi, with its spectacular complex of government buildings (1912-30).

Geddes was not impressed by this grandeur and he referred to New Delhi in scathing terms, finding it 'wholly un-spiritual'. Characteristically, his main criticism was of the low standard of workers' accommodation in the new city. Geddes preferred to dedicate his efforts mostly to the crowded Old Delhi, applying his methods of 'diagnostic survey' and 'conservative surgery' to improve the standard of living of the local population in the old town.

Frequently, Geddes found in India that the Administration's engineers had a tendency to cut straight new roads through the most congested urban areas. Implementation was often in the hands of officers untrained for the task who failed to realise the sociological aspects of the problem and whose views on hygiene and sanitation were based on European conventions. Most European settlers had found the congestion, noise and overcrowding too much for their families and ignoring the existing cities, preferred to build independent colonies for themselves at some remove. Military families were accommodated in 'cantonments', while officials and businessmen lived in 'civil lines'. Land in India was comparatively cheap and each bungalow could be given an acre or more of garden. The 'compounds' thus formed also housed servants and their families. These were numerous since domestic service was done mostly by men (women were prevented from working other than as *ayahs* or children's nurses) and the caste system prevented a man from doing more than one kind of work.

Geddes tackled the problem of cities with quite a different approach. His 'diagnostic survey' sought to unravel the old city labyrinths in order to find out how they had grown up and to identify the forces underlying their development and their eventual decay. With this understanding he would turn the very difficulties into opportunities, putting into practice his method of 'conservative surgery' developed in Edinburgh at the turn of the century. This consisted in demonstrating that the expensive and intrusive new roads of the engineers were rarely needed. Instead, he recommended the removal of only the most dilapidated and insanitary houses, conservatively and selectively – enough to allow light and air in every remaining house and to permit sanitation. By this method, and simply by enlarging existing lanes and creating small open spaces for inner city gardens, for meeting and for play, he would achieve better overall results – at a fraction of the cost of major works, and with a minimal disruption to the communities.

Fig 7 shows, on the left, the detailed nature of a Geddes survey in an Indian city. The straight lines show the intentions of the city engineers – compare

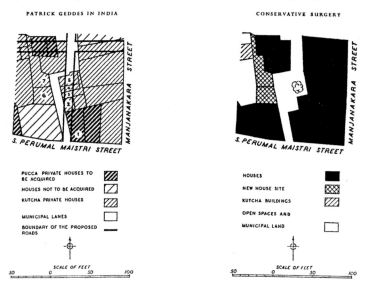

Fig 7 Conservative surgery in an Indian city, Madura.
A micro-study, before and after. First, survey (Sympathy), then the plan (Synthesis).
(*Patrick Geddes in India*, Jaqueline Tyrwhitt, 1947)

Haussmann in Paris or Abercrombie in Edinburgh. On the Geddes plan note the untidy mix of old and new and the individuality of this little area – down to the planting of a single tree to shade the newly-created community 'square'.

This concern for detail is shown in Fig 8, where someone, probably Arthur Geddes, has come up with designs for workers' houses. The setting is a town gate at Indore, with a lively sketch and a simple plan below.

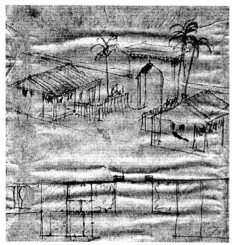

Fig. 8 Indore – pencil sketch of planned workers' houses.

Probably by Arthur Geddes. A town gate with plan of houses (below) and a sketch, complete with trees.

(Patrick Geddes Archive, University of Edinburgh)

In contrast with their Delhi experience, Patrick and Alasdair fell in love with Benares (now Varanasi). (See Plates 2a) and 2b)). I am not surprised. I found myself fascinated on arrival by 'this wonderful old city of religion'. You can wander in awe through lanes lined with temples and shrines leading down to the 'cosmic river', the sacred Ganges and its bathing *ghats*. Told that the best way to see the city was at sunrise from the river, we got up early the next day and found, even in the dark, great activity along the steps down to the river's edge. It was already full of people praying, bathing or making offerings to the river in little floating vessels with flowers and lighted candles. Soon, and still in total darkness, we were taken in a small row-boat silently to the middle of the river. The only light came from the 'burning ghats' where bodies are ritually cremated in funeral pyres and their ashes scattered in the Ganges. Suddenly, the city facing east over the river, you begin to see the town's outline in silhouette and the sky becomes all tinged with pink and orange, reflected in the river. There is an eerie silence for a place that is teeming with people. Gradually the light falls on the lofty turrets of the high palaces, then on the shrines by the riverbank, some partly collapsed and half buried by the force of the river. A truly uplifting experience!

We had to agree with Geddes when he described at Benares his 'great relief to find yourself in a world where ideas and meditations on them are recognised as the main business of life'.

He finds 'architecture and art frankly at the service of a religion, with hygiene at its base and poetry at its origins'. Geddes's vivid descriptions of Benares shows how much this city had affected him:

'Benares is a medley of architecture and life, of colour and verdure, of palace and ruin, of temples and shrines, of life-death, the like of which is nowhere else to be seen'.

On his second visit, Geddes travelled between Calcutta, Lucknow and Darjeeling. He was, at the time, organising a Summer Meeting in Darjeeling, helped as usual by his wife Anna. But his third season in India was to be one of disappointment, illness and finally bereavement in its most tragic form. It was in Calcutta that Anna Morton, Patrick's wife, died of enteric fever, contracted earlier at Lucknow Hospital where she had gone to get over a bout of dysentery. Just before her death, Geddes learned that his son Alasdair had been killed in action in France during the Great War. Patrick, told that the sad news would be too much for Anna to bear, had to keep the pain to himself, reading to Anna Alasdair's last letters, still arriving in the post.

I visited Calcutta in 1998. There is so much to take in that even a long stay would be insufficient to begin to understand this teeming metropolis. It was here that Anna died and Geddes heard of Alasdair's death. With these thoughts in mind, I followed my guide, an academic and professional planner involved in the restoration of Geddes plan of the *Burrah Bazaar* in the overcrowded city centre. Geddes had applied there the same principles as for regeneration in Edinburgh, a strategy of restoration, rehabilitation, conservative surgery and also new development.

In a tropical environment such as Calcutta's, nature has a tendency to take over. It was difficult to identify the original area of Geddes time and the network of open spaces that he tried to create there, as in Edinburgh, in order to provide breathing spaces for the local people. Even new buildings are soon covered in vegetation sprouting in roofs and from any cracks. Besides, in India there is a strong tendency for private encroachment onto any available public space. This is why he insisted in planting trees in the newly opened garden space to avoid their being thus encroached.

I had heard so much about Calcutta from my mentor Percy Johnson-Marshall, a great follower of Patrick Geddes. Percy had been posted there during the Second World War, his regiment being based for what proved a lengthy period in the city, awaiting orders to advance into Burma. Percy, born in Adjmer, had a very close affinity with India. His father was in the British administration and he grew up in India until he and his brother were sent to a boarding school in England. At Calcutta, Percy set out to create a Social Union on the lines of the Social Union of Edinburgh, where Geddes and his wife Anna had been active to help the poorer inhabitants of the Old Town improve their conditions. It was in Calcutta that Percy met April, his second wife. April had come from Argentina as a volunteer nurse and became very active also in the Calcutta Social Union. Percy and April are still remembered fondly by many people there especially among a group of artists, poets, painters and singers, followers of Tagore and Geddes. I was privileged to meet some of them thanks to an introduction from April. In Calcutta, Professor Geddes, Professor Percy Johnson-Marshall – and Edinburgh – are firmly associated together.

Percy is remembered in particular for his series of lectures on planning principles, which he broadcast by radio from an army barracks. These ten lectures formed the seed which was to grow into the programme for the Urban Design and Regional Planning Department at the University of Edinburgh. During the years under Percy Johnson-Marshall, the Department afforded to several hundred postgraduate students representing some 85 different countries from all over the world an education in planning based centrally on the ideas and methods of Patrick Geddes. No wonder then that Geddes is still more widely known abroad than in Edinburgh!

My third encounter with 'Geddes in India' was in Lahore, Pakistan. I have visited Lahore at intervals, accompanying my husband who was directing an academic link in planning with the University of Engineering and Technology of Lahore.

Lahore impresses the imagination. A city of palaces, great tombs, and an extraordinary Fort, it had risen from its mediaeval origins to become one of the capitals of the Moghul Empire, favoured particularly by the Emperor Jehangir. At its core lies the ancient and very beautiful Walled City. Nearby stands the grand Badshahi Mosque, built by the Emperor Aurangzeb in 1673, its majestic domes and minarets dominating the skyline (see Plate 3a).

When Geddes went to Lahore in 1917, he would have visited the Museum created by John Lockwood Kipling, father of Rudyard Kipling. This is where the story of 'Kim' begins: the famous *Zamzama* gun still stands guard at the Museum door. He would have also followed the elder Kipling's *Guide Book of Lahore*, published in 1876.

I had with me a copy of Geddes's report on Lahore, but no early 20th century overall map, and it was by no means easy to locate the areas in which Geddes had proposed action, let alone to trace actual implementation. Places and buildings changed names after Partition and documentation is now largely inaccessible to scholars. I located the basement room at the Municipality where pre-Partition documents were kept. It was an overwhelming sight. There, piled from floor to ceiling, thousands of documents and files lay neatly tied in red ribbons. Where to start looking? There was no list available: the Municipality has no staff to deal with documents of the British period. I went too to search in the University Library. It was not easy there for me either, perhaps because I am a woman.

While in Lahore, and in order to avoid any problems, I wore Pakistani dress, *shalwar kameez* complete with veil, but this did not make much difference. Men and women are largely segregated in education. Libraries, and specially archives, are organised mainly for men, there being a special reading room for women only. The few women students of Planning at the University that I met in Lahore were eager to talk to me and tell me of these and many other difficulties due to their gender. I had to admire their courage in pursuing a degree. I come from a supposedly quite 'macho' culture, but I had never encountered such conditions in South America. No wonder Geddes was adamant that women's education level was an important indication of a country's stage of development and that it was paramount to improve the standard of women's education in order to raise a society's true standard of living.

I finally located Geddes's proposed suburb south of Lahore near the Canal. It is now one of the most desirable places to live in town. Unfortunately, it is only available now for well-to-do or high ranking government officials' families. It is a classic 'Garden Suburb' layout with wide avenues and generous garden space. It includes a very fine park, now Bagh-i-Jinnah, formerly Lawrence Gardens, and, alongside the Government Officials' Residences or GOR estate. It has also a zoological garden, a racecourse and a polo ground. The Garden Suburb plan was signed, as always, by the local administrator, but on turning the paper two small letters were visible on the corner: 'PG'. I knew then that Geddes had been there. Geddes recommended in his report that, although money was not then available to implement the plan fully, priority should be given to the planting of trees along the planned lines of the subdivision avenues. He instructed municipal officials to spend their restricted budget on tree planting before even the necessary infrastructure of water and sewerage.

Geddes found the cost of tree planting to be a frequent source of objection in India. In his contribution, Walter Stephen suggests that Gandhi's imperfect understanding of the importance of trees may have contributed to Geddes's less than total admiration for him. PG recommended that every city establish a municipal tree nursery:

'Good large pits for the trees, containing good soil enriched with road sweepings; careful watering for two or three years; and the selection of a good foreman interested in his work'.

How right he was. The trees in his garden suburb in Lahore are now fully matured. The tree-lined avenues, now properly finished with side walks and road surfaces, would not look out of place in any leafy suburb of a European city.

In Lahore, Geddes also recommended clearing a much needed open square at the heart of the crowded Walled City (Plate 3c), fronting the Wazir Khan mosque (in the drawing below, the close shading represents an inchoate mass of housing, impossible to map accurately) (Plate 3b). It was disappointing to see this project had been only partly implemented, had been quite unfinished and was now much encroached upon. It struck me that Geddes's scheme would be as valid today as it was a century ago. It was here too incidentally that he condemned the mess of overhead electrical and telegraph cables. They are still

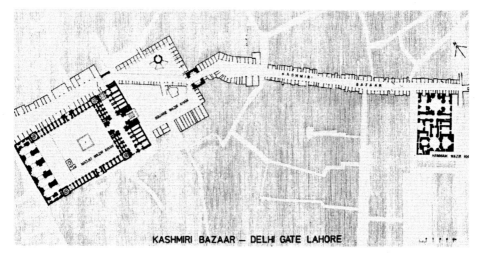

Fig 9 Lahore – Opening up the Mosque to the City
The Delhi Gate is off to the right. A bazaar/street is to be opened up to give a
worthy access route to the Wazir Khan Square and the Mosque beyond. The close
shading indicates dense and impenetrable housing.
(Patrick Geddes Archive, University of Edinburgh)

there and I wholly agreed with him that if the cables could be buried under-
ground and their brutal supports scrapped, the city's great buildings could be
seen again in their original grandeur.

Several years later, I went to India again. This time I was invited to visit
the city of Patiala by Gurmeet Rai, a young and talented Indian architect married
to the well-known photographer Raghu Rai. Gurmeet had come to Edinburgh
to take a refresher course on stone and lime construction. She was working on
the restoration of the *Qila* or fort of Patiala – a counterpart to our own
Edinburgh Castle. The *Qila* of Patiala is an impressive stone building, but had
deteriorated due to lack of maintenance and some parts had actually collapsed.
During the course of her work for the Indian National Trust (INTACH), Gurmeet
found that there was a Plan for the city by Sir Patrick Geddes. She came to
the Outlook Tower and spent some time at what by now was the Patrick
Geddes Centre for Planning Studies. I was then Director of the Centre and of
its archival collection, following the illness and death of its founder, Percy
Johnson-Marshall.

I was soon invited to take a copy of Geddes's Patiala report to the present
Maharajah who is very interested in the regeneration of the Punjabi capital.
I remember a comfortable, air conditioned, train from Delhi to Patiala, and
the endless green fields with huge mango trees marking property borders. The
plain of Punjab is one of the most fertile areas of India. We enjoyed generous

hospitality in the Maharajah's palace, accommodated very comfortably in two suites of rooms with a common lounge. This was not the same palace where Patrick and Arthur stayed in 1922, but a 1960s building with all modern facilities and set in extensive grounds with well kept gardens.

We were given all facilities during our stay including a car and driver. Gurmeet, who, as a working mother, had brought along her two year-old daughter and her *ayah*, was a great guide. By Indian standards, Patiala is a small city even though it is a provincial capital. We had the Geddes report with us and it was wonderful to have to hand Geddes's impressions as we visited the sites. After the first explorations, we decided to leave the official vehicle and take to the more usual local transport – a rickshaw. In a town where the majority of the people are pedestrians, a car is often a hindrance rather than a help. The rickshaw however, is non-polluting, less intrusive than the car and certainly less socially divisive. You feel among the people in the street and yet are just enough above their heads to be able to appreciate buildings and monuments! You can do everything from a rickshaw, including shopping, without coming down from it.

The copy of the Geddes report was duly given to the Maharajah and now, several years later, there is a strong move to promote a Patiala-Edinburgh link. Among Geddes's other influential contacts in the East was that with Baha'u Allah (1817-1892), the religious leader born in Teheran and founder of the Baha'i faith. An active chapter of the faith dates from Baha's visit to Edinburgh where Geddes invited him to give a lecture at the Outlook Tower. Geddes met also the philosopher from Calcutta, Swami Vivekananda (1862-1902), formerly known as Narendranath Datta and founder of the Raja Yoga movement. A leading disciple of Rama Krishna, he attempted to combine Indian spirituality with western materialism.

For Geddes, born and first educated in the Scottish Presbyterian tradition, contact with eastern beliefs contributed to widening his views and philosophical outlook. This was not fully appreciated by members of the Edinburgh establishment who did not see kindly, indeed became alarmed, at the presence at the Outlook Tower of theosophists, occultists, reformers and anarchists. This might explain why Geddes was never fully accepted in Edinburgh!

Palestine

After the Great War Palestine became a British Mandate under the Balfour Declaration. The period of the Mandate in Palestine, however controversial now, was a remarkable period for planning. Distinguished planners, British and others, were invited either by the government or by the Zionist movement, among them McLean, Ashbee, Kauffmann, Abercrombie, the Edinburgh architect Frank Mears – and of course Patrick Geddes. The political difficulties of the future were not fully envisaged; on the contrary, the prevailing mood was one of great enthusiasm at the promise of immense opportunities.

The ideas of the Garden City Movement had come to dominate planning at the time and they were quickly accepted. There was, however, an awareness that planning and building in Palestine was different from any other place. Rehabilitation and restoration work assumed especial significance and new buildings too took on intense messianic undertones. Planners were full of enthusiasm for the New Jerusalem and for reconstructing the Land of Israel. There were however practical problems too. Often Geddes, like Abercrombie or Mears, could only stay working in Palestine for some few weeks, or at the most some months at a time, and had to run the rest by correspondence. Geddes stopped several times in Palestine *en route* to and from India.

Patrick Geddes's Plan for Tel Aviv of 1925 envisaged a model 'city of gardens'. It described his vision as 'a new type of civic grouping, at once more beautiful and more health giving than any previous form of community in human annals'. It was indeed an exceptional design based on comprehensive city planning guided by social vision and awareness of habitat. The Geddes Plan was officially accepted in 1926 and was to be arguably the most fully implemented of any of Geddes's city plans. It established the overall structure of Tel Aviv, now a big metropolis and the financial and commercial capital of Israel.

But the greatest commission would have been for Jerusalem. The immensely complex ethnic mix, and the rehabilitation needs of the ancient city suited Geddes ability and inclinations, but not the political power struggle. In the event Geddes finished only a preliminary report for the city's development. Geddes also asked Frank Mears to help with the design of the University of Jerusalem but only the Library was completed.

Afterword

Geddes is sometimes accused of 'empiricism' or of lacking in method. He was, in fact, a very rigorous thinker, working as he did for the systematisation of the sciences. He did not set out to design a theoretical concept and method of planning. However, this is in effect what he did, and before going on to put his ideas into practice, he worked out for himself a dynamic model for action – one which he went on refining every time he tested it against a given reality.

He did not leave a formula or a set way of doing things, but a conceptual, constantly evolving model to be tested by practitioners and to be constantly adjusted, refined and modified. Hence the permanence and importance of his sequence: 'Survey-Analysis-Plan'. The sequence, always acknowledged, but never fully described or published, is based on Geddes's belief that humanity, being part of the natural world, should therefore follow the same core rules of nature as do other organisms – even bacteria or protozoa. Only the scales are different, and the complexities and levels of interaction are increased, when it comes to the relationship between man and his environment.

Man is the Organism, but the Environment around him is both natural and man-made. Man is affected by his environment and at the same time the environment can be, and is, profoundly affected by man. The conscious interaction of man and his environment is, therefore, essential to Geddes's model.

Geddes was to insist constantly, wherever his activities took him, on raising the consciousness of the human group, starting from childhood. Planning for him was the gentle but purposeful guiding of this interaction between man and the environment towards a desired goal. The key to achieve this goal is the conscious participation of people affected by planning action. Public participation is not the 'icing on the cake', but is at the very core of planning.

Patrick Geddes: Environment and Culture
Murdo Macdonald

THIS ESSAY STEMS FROM thinking I began in earnest about fifteen years ago, and many people – from places as diverse as Yamaguchi, Bengal and Berlin – have helped me to develop the ideas in the intervening period. I owe a particular recent debt to Ninian Stuart and the Trustees of the Falkland Heritage Trust, for allowing me to explore some of the thinking outlined here in a lecture at House of Falkland in Fife. My other immediate debt is to Walter Stephen of the Sir Patrick Geddes Memorial Trust, for a number of constructive and significant additions to my text. To all those concerned I commend Geddes's motto: 'by creating we think'.

This year marks the 150th anniversary of the birth of Patrick Geddes. He was Professor of Botany at University College Dundee from 1888 to 1919. But he is remembered today not only as a biologist, but as a geographer, an ecologist, an arts activist, a pioneer of community-based town planning and an international educator. We can regard the two intertwined strands of the regeneration and sustaining of environment on the one hand and of the revival and sustaining of culture on the other as fundamental to all Geddes's thinking. He saw these two strands of activity – environmental and cultural – as completely interdependent and his life was an exploration of that interdependence and an attempt to convey its importance to others.

As a biologist Geddes was absorbed by the study of living things. Exploring Kinnoull Hill from an early age, working in the garden of Mount Tabor Cottage with his father, and wandering further afield, all contributed to his love of the beauty of the natural world and his admiration of its complexity. In early adulthood his near blindness in Mexico thrust upon him the necessity to rethink his life so that, instead of knowing more and more about less and less, he took upon himself the responsibility of studying human beings in their environment, not merely in academic terms, but as a prelude to action, to making things better.

For Geddes every issue was a spur to interdisciplinary action. The biologist was still present when a question prompted a regional survey, the findings were analysed and the plan produced. Then synergy began. Thus a garden became not only an excuse for healthy occupation in the open air, producing extra food or beautiful flowers and cheering up the locality, it was an outdoor laboratory for the study of life forms and the seasons. Furthermore, Geddes's gardens were located in the community and this meant allocation of responsibilities: purchases, maintenance and all the minutiae of a community enterprise – in fact, good training for democratic action.

Geddes's attitudes to culture can also be traced back to his early life. His upbringing in a Free Kirk home ensured a consistent exposure to words, to the riches of the Bible and the subtleties of the sermon. We can be sure that Sunday afternoons would involve the re-examination and teasing out of the morning sermon while Bible reading would have been regular. Indeed Geddes was to draw heavily on both the Bible and John Bunyan's *Pilgrim's Progress* as teaching tools in his adult work.

Although Geddes's prose style is open to criticism, when it is problematic the difficulties usually stem from Geddes being verbally overambitious. To wit, attempting to get too much meaning into the compass of one sentence. By contrast his general ability to use words with notable effect is clear in his concise descriptions of a process – 'conservative surgery' – or a method – 'impact anonymous'. 'Conurbation' and 'megalopolis' may be the only Geddes-created words to be in frequent use today, but he was always able to conjure up a new word or redefine an old one to stimulate thought.

After leaving Perth Academy at the age of fifteen – and reflecting an unusually liberal attitude on the part of his parents – Patrick had several years of varied and informal further education, under the overall guidance of his father. This included cabinet making, and this activity seems to have profoundly influenced his belief in practical things and the balanced education of head, hand and heart, domains which we might now call cognitive, psychomotor and affective. For Geddes the making of a box was to be the perfect example of an integrated educational experience. He also attended a local art class in Perth, where he showed a high degree of competence in representational drawing.

But his real visual talent lay in analytical sketches and the representation of complex thought in two-dimensional form, what he called his 'thinking machines', notably the remarkable *Notation of Life*.

He appreciated visual thinking in all its forms, and wrote frequently about art (focusing more on the content than the form), which he valued for its ability to enrich the human spirit. Indeed, when he was working with Thomas Huxley in London, he took a month off to go round galleries. He also valued art as a

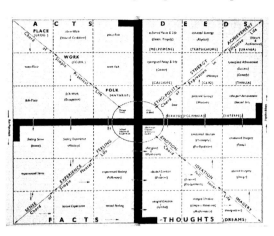

Fig. 10 A Geddes 'Thinking Machine' –
The Notation of Life.

(*The Interpreter Geddes: The Man and His Gospel*, Amelia Defries, 1927).

means of teaching using perception in concert with the intellect: 'one in the eye is worth ten in the ear' as they used to say in colleges of education.

Furthermore, he acted as a patron commissioning book illustrations and designs for his publishing projects, and murals and stained glass for specific locations such as halls of residence and the Outlook Tower. These works were always pedagogic in intent, whether the subject was Celtic myth, Scottish history, or the geography of the region.

By marrying Anna Morton in 1886 Geddes ensured that there would be classical music around him. Anna had studied music and singing in Dresden and music became part of the home education of the Geddes children. Each learned a different instrument – Norah, piano, Alasdair piano, then cello, Arthur, violin – and there were regular family recitals. In the evenings after Geddes's pioneering interdisciplinary summer schools Anna gave recitals. Also involved was Marjory Kennedy Fraser, who would go on to perform a key role in the Celtic revival as collector and arranger of Hebridean folk songs. Walter Stephen (whose help with this introductory section I gratefully acknowledge, and who, at the time of writing, is chair of the Sir Patrick Geddes Memorial Trust) recalls a meeting of the Edinburgh University Geography Society in about 1961. About a hundred students were assembled when the speaker failed to turn up. Unperturbed, Arthur Geddes, then teaching at the university, handed round copies of his own collection of Scottish songs, *Songs of Craig and Ben*, tuned up his fiddle and led this mass of students 'on the verge of Beatlemania' in an hour of exuberant music and singing. What better indication could there be of Patrick Geddes's own concern with cultural matters, than this demonstration by a member of his family?

Although Geddes had a lack of classical music in his life prior to his marriage to Anna Morton, it should not be thought that music as a whole was absent from his life prior to that date. With a father in the Black Watch, it is no surprise to discover Geddes's lifelong commitment to the music of the Highland bagpipe. Indeed this interest resulted in a mural scheme on the history of pipe music (Highland and otherwise) painted by John Duncan for the Geddes family flat in the 1890s.

It is easy to see the pipes as merely a stereotypical icon of Scottishness, but that is to ignore the range and sophistication of its music, for example, its scale unique to the music of the West. Geddes was well aware both of the stereotype and of the sophistication, and when his son Alasdair was thirteen, he wrote to him suggesting that he take up the instrument, taking over two pages to give his reasons. It is interesting to note that the reasons given were not musical but cultural – the courage of the piper in battle, the effects of the pipes on social occasions, dancing, weddings, funerals, tales of old magic, etc. Patrick continues:

'in a summer or two you will lead some of our excursions, and almost from the first you will be able to start the march and help the fun'.

A grainy old photograph shows the children of Castlehill School marching down to the official opening of their new garden, led by Alasdair and the pipes. It is significant that Geddes should have favoured an instrument so uniquely Scottish, which touched Scottish culture at so many points and which is eminently suitable for the grand occasion in the open air.

Geddes had a passion for creating meeting places for discussing ideas and just bringing people together. These meeting places included the informal colleges of his halls of residence in Edinburgh and London, his pioneering summer schools in Edinburgh and Paris, and towards the end of his life his Scots College in Montpellier. He referred to one of these meeting places, the Outlook Tower in Edinburgh, as an 'index of indexes', a kind of encyclopaedic meta-view of all available knowledge. Zueblin, the professor from Chicago, called this same Outlook Tower 'the world's first sociological laboratory'. That may be accurate, but for Geddes this index of indexes, this sociological laboratory was first and foremost a meeting place open to all.

Geddes's environmental side can be introduced through his last lecture to his students in Dundee delivered in 1919, before he left to take up the chair of Civics and Sociology at the University of Bombay. He made this concise statement of his ecological vision:

'How many people think twice about a leaf? Yet the leaf is the chief product and phenomenon of Life: this is a green world, with animals comparatively few and small, and all dependent upon the leaves. By leaves we live. Some people have strange ideas that they live by money. They think energy is generated by the circulation of coins. Whereas the world is mainly a vast leaf-colony, growing on and forming a leafy soil, not a mere mineral mass: and we live not by the jingling of our coins, but by the fullness of our harvests.'

This wonderful paragraph was reported by Amelia Defries in her pioneering biography of Geddes published in 1927. Interestingly, the Ballater Geddes Group have chosen as their motto 'By Leaves We Live', rather than the more obvious 'Vivendo Discimus' (By Living We Learn).

Typically enough, one of PG's greatest contributions to the arts has a most environmental title, namely his

Fig. 11 Helen Hay – Almanac
(The Evergreen Book of Summer, 1896)

Plate 1a
Milne's Court
(as renovated by the Saltire Society in 1971)

Plate 1b
Geddes Ceiling in Riddle's Court
(celebrating student achievement)

Plate 1c
Witches' Well
(on the site of 17th century burnings)

Plate 2a
Benares (Varanasi) – Palaces

Plate 2b
Benares (Varanasi) – The Ganges

Plate 3a
Lahore – Profile from public park

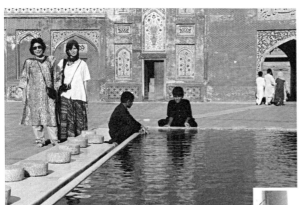

Plate 3b
Lahore – Wazir Khan Mosque
(central court with
purification tank)

Plate 3c
Lahore – old houses

Plate 4a
Valley Section – Stained Glass Panel
(the most elaborate version of Geddes's simple model)

Plate 4b
Detail of Panel

Plate 4c
Detail of Panel

Plate 4d
Detail of Panel

Plate 4e
Detail of Panel

Plate 5a
Mount Tabor Cottage, Perth
(the Geddes family home)

Plate 5b
Kinnoull Hill from the south
(a formative influence on Geddes)

Plate 6a
The 'Old Academy'
attended by Geddes
in the 'New Town' of
Perth

Plate 6b
Blythe's Tower at 184
metres
(a local 'Outlook Tower'
near Kinglassie)

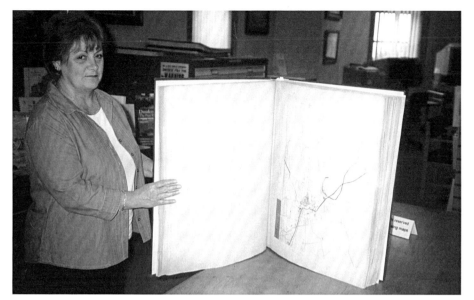

Plate 7a
Norman Johnson's Dunfermline Survey of 1946

Plate 7b
The Dragons of
Wardrop's Court

Plate 7c
'It's comin' yet for a' that' – Ramsay Garden
(a sermon in stone)

Plate 8a
Johnston Terrace Garden in 2004
(compare Figs. 2 and 3)

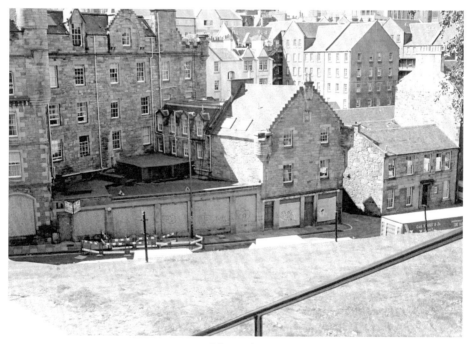

Plate 8b
Regenerating the Regenerated Old Town
(a challenge for the 21st Century)

magazine *The Evergreen* published in 1895 and 1896. At one and the same time *The Evergreen* evokes ecology and cultural revival, indeed it refers directly back to Allan Ramsay's eighteenth-century collection of poetry of the same name. Each issue began with an almanac recording the passing of the seasons, beautiful works of art, for the most part by Helen Hay, reflecting directly on nature.

Geddes's cultural contribution can be emphasised through the words of the art historian Duncan Macmillan. In 1994 he wrote of 'the belief expressed so forcefully by Patrick Geddes a hundred years ago that art is part of a nation's vitality and a measure of its well-being; it should be modern and international in its horizons, but it should also be the product of a nation's own values, of its confidence in itself and of its awareness of its history.'

The Valley Section: Culture and Environment

Bringing together these two strands of Geddes's thinking, culture and environment, is one of his great diagrams or conceptual models, the deceptively simple Valley Section. This shows the course of a river from mountain to sea, and by extension, the habitats of human beings and the places of their cultures, their histories and their work. The diagram itself shows no river, but that is because the course of the river is itself Geddes's and our viewpoint.

Rivers were fundamental to Geddes's understanding, indeed, referring to his later experience in India, Geddes's biographer Philip Boardman wrote that 'the Ganges [reminded] him of his own childhood river, the Tay,' and he goes on to quote Geddes as saying of the Tay that it will always be 'for me my main impulse of the life-stream and of the cosmos'. Boardman continues to note Geddes's 'reminiscing about the fine views from the Kinnoull Hill cliffs,' again quoting Geddes that

'it must have been in the climbings and the ramblings over this fine valley landscape ... that I got the feeling of the valley section which has been a main vision of geography in later years',

This vision has wide applicability. Think, for example of the Valley Section as a model of the village of Falkland in the shadow of the Lomond Hills, with its watercourses irrigating the farmland of the plain of the Eden and eventually reaching the sea at that nexus of scholarship, religious turmoil, trade and fishing, namely St Andrews. Or again, think of the industrial and agricultural history of Scotland in terms of the wider Valley Section of one of our major rivers, the Clyde, from source to sea. The lead miners at Leadhills and Wanlockhead, the shepherds in the Lowther Hills, the fruit farms around Lanark, the steel mills of Lanarkshire, Renfrewshire and North Ayrshire, the shipyards of the upper and lower Clyde. It has been pointed out that the 'Song of the Clyde' is an exploration in popular song of precisely this Valley Section, and one can note that Smetana's orchestral tone poem *Vltava* echoes a Valley Section in Czech terms.

But the Lanarkshire lead mines are exhausted, steel and shipbuilding have all but vanished. Greater mobility in our times means that people no longer have to live beside their work, or work within walking distance of their homes. Glentress Forest, near Peebles, was one of the great forests planted post-1945 in an attempt to keep an active population in rural areas. Ten years ago, of the thirty-five people employed there, only one came from Peebles, the remainder commuted from Edinburgh! Does this mean that the Valley Section is obsolete or was never true? Not at all, for the mere fact that we are taking the model and testing it against a perceived reality is a demonstration of its purpose and value.

On a wider scale one can see the Valley Section as a model of the watersheds of Scotland as a whole, extending from the highland west to the lowland east, or indeed of Europe from the Alps to the Mediterranean or America from the Rockies to the Pacific. And Geddes was, of course, a great internationalist. Just as he traversed the boundaries between subjects he traversed the boundaries between nations. Boardman wrote that 'with the approach of the twentieth century [Geddes] placed himself [in a category] of world citizenship ...' More concisely Geddes's self-declared disciple, Lewis Mumford, wrote that 'Geddes's Scotland embraced Europe and his Europe embraced the world.' And this is how one should see the Valley Section, as a diagram of global relevance.

The Valley Section appears in several forms. The most colourful, the most complex, and one of the most illuminating versions is the stained glass panel which Geddes commissioned for the Outlook Tower in Edinburgh in the 1890s (see Plate 4a). Some other versions, often drawn after Geddes's death, can be too simple, too clear, perhaps suggesting, wrongly, inevitable cause and effect. But as we have already seen, the Valley Section deals in possibilities, not certainties. In the Outlook Tower panel meant for public display, Geddes can be seen making sense of basic human activities with respect to the appropriate place for those activities – hunting in the forest, shepherding on the hill, mining within the hill, crofting on the low land, market gardening on the outskirts of the city, fishing in the sea and trade across its surface. Crucially, this is not just a simple diagram of the basic activities that allow us to live and clothe ourselves. Geddes glosses his visual text with Latin phrases:

'*Microcosmos Naturae. Sedes Hominum. Theatrum Historiae. Eutopia Futuris*'.

He is insisting that we look again at the valley from a set of contrasting and yet mutually illuminating viewpoints.

The valley is first and foremost for Geddes the biologist a 'microcosm of nature' (Plate 4b). For Geddes, if we want to understand the biology of our planet, we start in the microcosm of our own locality. From, for example, the tributaries of the Eden flowing from the Lomonds via Falkland to St Andrews we can move to the Tay flowing from Rannoch Moor via Perth to Dundee.

Or to the courses of Rhine and Danube as they define the European land-mass. And from there let us think more widely of, for example, the Ganges flowing from the mountains of the Himalayas to Calcutta. Here indeed the Valley Section can be seen as a microcosm of nature that can be scaled up from the local into a macrocosmic understanding of the essential relationships of water and earth that underpin the sustainability of the planet.

But alongside the '*microcosmos naturae*', this same river valley defines the '*sedes hominum*' that is to say the abode of human beings (Plate 4c), the place where people are born, live their lives, have their memories and die. A microcosm of nature still, but developing into a model of society and its culture and institutions also. Geddes emphasises this in his next phrase in which the river valley is conceived of as a dramatic '*theatrum historiae*', a theatre of history (Plate 4d). Here the move from the environmental emphasis on the valley to the cultural emphasis is firmly made. We have already touched on this drama of history in terms of the post-industrial changes around the Clyde, referred to earlier. It is equally straightforward to consider such a vision of the Valley Section in terms of places like Falkland or Perth, St. Andrews or Edinburgh, Glasgow or Inverness. And not only through the realities of archaeology and history, but through the creative reimaginings of architects, artists, poets and novelists. For Geddes it is only through the understanding of history and all its related disciplines, as they apply to particular locations, that we can look in a clear sighted way to the future. So we move to his next motto '*eutopia futuris*' (Plate 4e).

This, finally, is the 'eutopia' or 'good place' of the future. Not the 'utopia' with a 'u' by which Sir Thomas More implied an idealised 'no place' but 'eutopia' with an 'eu', a good place that Geddes believed could be achieved through local and international co-operation. But note that Geddes offers us an alternative to the 'eutopia' of the future, namely the 'kakatopia' or bad place of the future. He knows that we have a choice between ruining the planet and enabling it to sustain itself. Remember his words

'this is a green world, with animals comparatively few and small, and all dependent upon the leaves. By leaves we live.'

Older people among us grew up in a world where it was assumed that, if more food were needed, all we had to do was to find new fishing grounds, plough up new land, bring in more water or apply more fertiliser. Over a century ago, Geddes was clear sighted in realising the limitations of such views. His clear sight does him credit today, but at the same time we are humbled by realising how long we have ignored his environmental message.

Yet the information in Geddes's window does not stop there. Looking at the window we note that the microcosm of nature – with its suggestions of a more primitive, immediately nature-dependent way of life – is linked to the idea of hunting through the flight of two game birds; whereas the theatre of history – with its implication of our present, institutionalised, historically-conscious, view of ourselves – seems to be represented by fighting birds of prey. At the same time the good place of the future, the 'eutopia', is symbolised by three doves flying in harmony. For Geddes, this latter transition was symbolic of a transition from a crudely mechanised society based on unfettered competition, to his dream of a society which made use of sophisticated, environmentally-friendly technologies, based on local and international co-operation. As we shall see later the three doves appear in many Geddes contexts and are usually said to represent 'sympathy', 'synthesis' and 'synergy'.

Geddes's eutopia would, he hoped, succeed the centralised and hierarchical power structure of his and our present. These are of course anarchist ideas – in the most constructive sense of that description – and they relate directly to Geddes's friendship with European anarchists of the day, in particular the Russian, Prince Peter Kropotkin and the Frenchman, Elisée Reclus, both of whom visited him in Edinburgh. These ideas also relate to his background in the Free Church of Scotland, an institution which gave him a taste both for wide-ranging intellectual debate and for minimal structures of government.

Anarchy and the Free Church

It is easy to stereotype the anarchists of Geddes's time as black-clad bomb-throwers and there were, indeed, a significant number of such people. Flipping over the pages of *Pageant of the Century*, published in 1933, one finds between 1900 and 1914 numerous assassinations and attempted assassinations of heads of state, royalty and influential politicians. For example in 1900 there was an attempt on the life of the Prince of Wales on a visit to Brussels, and the same year the King of Italy was killed. In 1904 the Russian minister of the interior was assassinated in St Petersburg. The next year there were attempts on the life of the Russian Tsar, the Sultan of Turkey and the King of Spain. And so on until in June 1914 a bomb exploded in Westminster Abbey, and in the same month Archduke Franz Ferdinand and his wife were assassinated at Sarajevo. Days before the troops of Europe were mobilised, Jaures, the Socialist, was shot dead by a young man in Paris.

So where did Geddes stand with respect to all of this? What interested Geddes about anarchy as a political philosophy was that it proposed a co-operative self-government based on a minimum of vested power. But he dissociates himself from 'mere fits of despairing hysterics and threats of dynamite'. Instead his anarchist friends were among the most thoughtful of geographers and social reformers. Prince Kropotkin was an advocate of self-help co-operation. He had heard of Geddes's early efforts of conservation and development of the urban fabric through community effort in James Court in Edinburgh's Old Town. In 1886, after his release from the French prison of Clairvaux,

Kropotkin made his way to Edinburgh, where he and Geddes found much to agree on. In 1917 Geddes was to say in a letter: 'I can but express my delight over the Russian Revolution. How glad I am old Kropotkin has lived to see this!'

Other anarchist associates of Geddes were the pioneering geographers Elisée Reclus and his brother Elie. Both were associated with the Paris Commune of 1871 but escaped the subsequent massacre by government troops. Instead they were sentenced to imprisonment on Devil's Island, but this sentence was changed to exile from France – following protests from eminent scientists in a number of countries. Both came to Edinburgh and Elisée, in particular, worked closely with Geddes. The attempt to create Elisée Reclus's giant globe showing the earth's surface in relief became something of an obsession for Geddes.

Paul Reclus, Elie's son, fled to Britain after the President of France was assassinated in Lyons and thirty anarchists were accused of forming a criminal association. Under the alias of 'George Guyou' he settled into the activities at the Outlook Tower, for example making a relief model of Edinburgh for Geddes to use. He occupied himself as a translator of technical works, but a booklet he published on the Dreyfus case, published by the Outlook Tower, ran into three editions. Later he followed Geddes to the Scots College in Montpellier where he became co-ordinator of studies, and assumed the role of director after Geddes's death.

Peter Hall in his *Cities of Tomorrow* comments that it was from 'Reclus and Kropotkin, and beyond them from Proudhon' that Geddes

'took his position that society had to be reconstructed not by sweeping governmental measures like the abolition of private property, but through the efforts of millions of individuals...' In other words – Think Global, Act Local.

For Geddes, his anarchism was European in reference but Scottish in its moral origin. In a letter Geddes underlines these Scottish ideological roots by making the surprising claim that Thomas Chalmers, the founder of the Free Kirk of Scotland in 1843, was an anarchist economist 'beside whom Kropotkin and Reclus are mere amateurs.' Geddes writes this in the context of his correspondent complaining to him about his positive use of the word 'anarchy'. He stoutly rebutted the criticism, although at the same time he makes clear that he has no intention of fully allying himself with anarchy, any more than with any other political philosophy. He does, however, make clear that he firmly believes in the desirability of the political state to which anarchy refers, namely that it 'simply means what it says an-archy – without government i.e. without governmental compulsion'. And, of course, it was such resistance to governmental compulsion that precipitated the foundation of the Free Church.

In the same letter, along with claiming Thomas Chalmers as an anarchist forebear, Geddes also makes clear his own commitment to the Free Church, asserting that it is the organisation of which he is 'proudest of all' to belong to. Geddes's stance has rightly been described as first and foremost 'a moralist, deeply concerned with bettering man and his lot' and Geddes's Free Church background is a crucial factor in this. It is only if one recognises this that one can make sense of Geddes's continuing and strong links with major Free Church figures, such as John Kelman, Alexander Whyte, and Whyte's wife Jane Barbour. With respect to Geddes, it is particularly important to emphasise the ecumenicism of the Free Church at this time. For example Alexander Whyte was on close terms with Cardinal Newman and published a selection of his writings, while his wife Jane was an early supporter of Baha'ism in Edinburgh, as was Geddes. Indeed, with his son-in-law Frank Mears, he produced a design for a Baha'i temple in 1922.

The Free Church was thus not only important to Geddes as a model of a minimal institutional structure, it was also a cultural guide. The Free Church at its foundation had attracted a strong group of intellectuals and artists and this has great relevance for an understanding of Geddes as a thinker. The Church had been founded in 1843, only eleven years before Geddes's birth, when about one third of the ministers of the Church of Scotland seceded. The background to this secession was the Patronage Act of 1712, by which parish ministers of the Church of Scotland were to be appointed by the local laird, regardless of the wishes of parishioners. Dissatisfaction with this led to a number of secessions over the next century or so, the largest being the Disruption of 1843 that led to the formation of the Free Church. The Disruption burnt itself into the folk memory of Scots Presbyterians and we can be sure that these then recent dramatic events were gone over time and time again in Geddes's childhood home in Perth.

This new church was brought into being not only by ministers, but by a body of Scotland's most significant thinkers. Among the lay founders was the St Andrews physicist Sir David Brewster. Brewster had been in 1831 a key figure in the British Association for the Advancement of Science. Another founder-member of the Free Church of Scotland was the painter David Octavius Hill, who painted an image of the Assembly which gave rise to the Free Church. Hill is best known for his pioneering role, along with Robert Adamson, in the development of portrait and social documentary photography, but began his collaboration with Adamson, at Brewster's suggestion, to help record the first General Assembly of the Free Church for his painting. But Hill had also been, since 1830, the very active secretary of the first body to properly represent the interests of professional artists in Scotland, namely the Scottish Academy (later the Royal Scottish Academy). Thomas Chalmers himself was the Academy's first chaplain, serving from 1830 until his death in 1847. Thus those who helped to bring the Free Church into being included those – like Chalmers, Brewster, and Hill – who had helped to structure and support major organisations concerned with both scientific research and artistic process. This conjunction of morality, spirituality, science and art, set the agenda for the young Patrick Geddes.

Other founders of the Free Kirk included the geologist and journalist Hugh Miller, Thomas Guthrie, the originator of the Ragged School movement, and the Greek scholar and Celtic revivalist John Stuart Blackie, who would directly inspire Geddes in his cultural work. Free Church figures of a younger generation, but still a decade or so older than Geddes, included Kropotkin's friend William Robertson Smith. Robertson Smith's social anthropological ideas were to influence not only his fellow Scot Sir James Frazer, but Geddes's close contemporaries the Austrian pioneer of psychoanalysis, Sigmund Freud and the English radical designer WR Lethaby. The link between Freud, Lethaby and Presbyterian thinkers in a Calvinist tradition like Smith and Frazer may seem somewhat surprising but perhaps it is less so when one notes the Calvinist background of the most mythologically inclined of all Freud's followers, CG Jung, indeed a Calvinist upbringing seems to have been a useful starting point from which to develop thinking about mythology in the latter half of the nineteenth century. Geddes's background in the Free Church thus provided him with a fertile thinking ground.

For example, William Robertson Smith's work on the status of the Bible as part of history rather than literal truth, had both helped to develop the emerging social science of anthropology, and also engendered a major debate within the Free Church. The outcome of the debate was that, in 1881, Smith narrowly lost his position as professor in the Free Church College at Aberdeen but at the same time he gained the editorship of the ninth edition of the then Edinburgh-based *Encyclopaedia Britannica*, to which Geddes was also a contributor. As a young man Geddes was well aware of the intricacies and ironies of the Robertson Smith affair, indeed he even considered – with some justification – that analogy with Robertson Smith's unfettered thinking had been used to undermine his own academic prospects.

Thus what one finds in the Free Church during this period is an institution which transcends the simple stereotype of 'stern Presbyterianism' which has been sometimes applied to Geddes's religious background. Indeed, one can conceive of it as an institution which facilitated a network of wide ranging debates on issues ranging from the status of legendary sources as history to the relationship of spiritual to temporal government.

Geddes and Generalism

So perhaps we should think of Geddes's three doves as Free Church doves of ecumenical and anarchist inclination. These three doves occur frequently on Geddes's publications from 1895 onwards. I am not sure who drew them: the likeliest candidate is John Duncan, not least because of his use of three birds in his *Apollo's Schooldays* in *The Evergreen: Book of Spring*, which seems to be also the first publication to use the three doves motif. However other artists of Geddes's milieu such as Helen Hay and Charles Mackie cannot be ruled out. The doves appear unexpectedly at first but then you start to look for them in books, on information sheets, etc. But for Geddes they were not just symbolic birds.

Fig. 12 Title Page from 'Dramatisations of History' (1923)

The three doves are much in evidence – not as a logo, but as a call to action. Not mentioned elsewhere is Geddes's interest in masques, pageants and other celebrations of community ('Folk'). This edition of *Dramatisations of History* (the 7th) was published in London, Edinburgh, Bombay and Karachi, printed in Madras and runs to 198 pages.
(*Dramatisations of History*, Patrick Geddes, 1923)

As I have noted the doves also represented three concepts: Sympathy, Synthesis and Synergy, and this message is thus also part of the Valley Section window. What Geddes meant by 'sympathy' was the enlightenment use of this word, the way Adam Smith used it, closer today to what we might call empathy, the ability to accurately imagine oneself in another's place. And from this sympathy, this emotional engagement with other people he proceeds to the intellectual power of comparing and synthesising different ideas. And finally, having emphasised first the emotional, and secondly the intellectual, he moves to the social notion of 'synergy', that is to say of acting together to solve problems and create opportunities – in other words Geddes's primary principle of successful human society, co-operation.

Thus in one image, the stained-glass version of the valley section diagram, Geddes provides the basis of a philosophy for thinking about human ecology, not only by drawing attention to the necessity of exploring any environment in terms of its natural characteristics, and the way in which those characteristics relate to the folk who live there and the work done, but also by specifying the psychological attitude necessary for any such analysis, that is to say an emotional, intellectual and co-operative engagement with that place, those folk and their work, to use one of Geddes's favourite combinations of terms.

If we look back over the twentieth century it becomes obvious that in terms of planning, whether we look north, south, east, or west, this simple interdependence of folk, work and place, and the engagement with these categories in terms of sympathy, synthesis and synergy, have too often been ignored. Geddes's three doves should not be seen as just a logo or a trademark. In fact they are a generalist manifesto for action.

I want to say some more about Geddes's generalism here. In making sense of the breadth of Geddes's vision we must note that he was a generalist thinker *par excellence*, and in this he is part of that wider Scottish educational tradition which George Davie has described as 'the democratic intellect'. In the 1960s Hugh MacDiarmid recalled that Geddes

'knew that watertight compartments are useful only to a sinking ship, and traversed all the boundaries of separate subjects.'

Quite so. Indeed Geddes's contemporary, the philosopher, classical scholar and educational theorist John Burnet, professor of Greek at the University of St Andrews, made an elegant statement of the value of such a generalist approach when he wrote of 'the most important side of any department of knowledge' as being 'the side on which it comes into contact with every other department'. Burnet's words could have been said by Geddes and this underlines the fact that in Geddes's generalism we find not an intellectually maverick trait unique to Geddes but the expression of an enduring interdisciplinary current in Scottish thought. It is this generalism that enabled Geddes to make pioneering contributions not only to biology, but also to town planning; not only to ecology, but also to the revival of communities through the agency of the arts.

In a similar vein to Burnet but speaking much more recently, the Italian architect Giancarlo De Carlo said:

'Specialisation, specialists, I consider in a way to be an accident of our present time. I think we should go back to the idea of the general view, and in Scotland you have a good grounding in this approach, not least because of the work of Patrick Geddes...'

The Valley as Place of Inner Being

A further aspect of Geddes's generalism can be registered if we think of the valley from the point of view of its potential as a mythological or legendary space. Lewis Mumford wrote that Olympus and Parnassus were as real to Geddes as protozoa, and perhaps this comment can give us a path to follow through the valley, not just as a place of biological, social and cultural evolution, but as a place of myth and inner being. The valley is not just an external drama of geology, biology and human history, it is a psychological drama of myth and legend.

Heinrich Zimmer wrote that:

'In dealing with symbols and myths from far away we are really conversing with ourselves – with part of ourselves, however, which is as unfamiliar to our conscious being as the interior of the earth to the students of geology. Hence the mythical tradition provides us with a map for exploring and ascertaining the contents of our own inner being to which we consciously feel only scantily related.'

Geddes would have agreed. If one looks at the Valley Section, even in its most minimal form, the aspects of the land to which Geddes draws our attention are as significant spiritually and mythologically as they are economically and ecologically. The hilltop, the forest, the mine, the field, the city, the sea; and of course the implied river, worthy of Neil Gunn, at the heart of the valley. One would of course expect the salient elements of an ecology of the planet to correspond with equally salient elements of an 'ecology of the mind', to use Gregory Bateson's phrase, but it further emphasises that in Geddes we have a consciousness of both the physical and the psychological aspects of landscape.

Geddes treats the mythical beings of the landscapes with great seriousness. Consider Geddes when he writes of the faerie folk of Celtic legend:

'There pass before us the Riders of the Sidhe, each offering one of the four gifts of life to men. First the leafing, flowering fruiting branch of the Life-Tree – the simple life and labour of the People. The next bears the cup – for the Joy of Life in its prosperity. The next is gazing into his magic crystal, of Thought; in which, from reflections from without, again from memories within, Emotion, Reason and Intuition are ever creating new visions. Finally comes the bearer of the Sword – for Idealism in Action, Justice in Rule.' This scene was illustrated very exactly in 1911 by Geddes's colleague, the painter John Duncan whose *Riders of the Sidhe* is an intriguing work of Celtic revival symbolist art, which is today part of the art collection of the city of Dundee.

Note how Geddes makes use of these legendary beings to make points about thought and action. Not for nothing did his own nickname 'the interpreter' come from that great teaching text, Bunyan's *Pilgrim's Progress*. He is acutely conscious of the importance of the legendary for the everyday and vice versa. In this sense one finds in Geddes a closeness to the mythological writers of Scotland, from William Robertson Smith and James Frazer through Andrew Lang to Donald A Mackenzie and Lewis Spence; and of course this spirit of the age, of which Geddes was part, found its literary expression in the works of, among others, George MacDonald, Robert Louis Stevenson and JM Barrie.

One finds strong echoes of it in literature of the twentieth century in the work not only of Hugh MacDiarmid, but of Neil Gunn, Alasdair Gray and Edwin Morgan. South of the Border – via George MacDonald – it leads to CS Lewis. Via John Duncan's friend William Craigie, it leads to JRR Tolkien. Across the Atlantic, through Geddes's friend the art historian and cultural activist Ananda Coomaraswamy, we find a direct link to America's great advocate of the everyday importance of myth, Joseph Campbell.

Geddes knew that any valley anywhere in the world would have its appropriate myth system – Greek, Hindu, Buddhist, Celtic or whatever – and that these in turn would relate to one another. He makes this relational point when he writes, for example, of the interplay of Norse, Classical and Celtic deities:

'Angus Og, the God of Youth, in whom the characters of Dionysos, of Apollo, of Balder the Beautiful, all mingle and meet.'

On the one hand Geddes respected the cultural integrity of myth systems, on the other hand he recognised not only their links but also their usefulness as ways of thinking, ways of coding ideas, sometimes matching one another, sometimes complementing one another. At the watershed of the valley we may find, perhaps, Parnassus or the Hill of Tara or Mount Meru or Mount Tabor or, indeed, the faerie hill of the Caledonians – Schiehallion. Geddes recognised these mythological complexes, of which these mountains are part, as a language for use. He had an immediate understanding of what Jung called the archetypal. So when Lewis Mumford said that Olympus and Parnassus were as real to Geddes as protozoa, he meant it.

Mumford's point is that all our realities whether cultural or environmental were valued equally by Geddes. It is this capacity to appreciate the wholeness of human experience and the interdependence of all parts of that experience that gives Geddes his greatness as a thinker and an activist.

Patrick Geddes: Regional Survey and Education

Kenneth Maclean

Introduction

DURING HIS LIFE AND career, Patrick Geddes (1854-1932) nailed his colours to a variety of masts: biology, sociology, planning, conservation, Celtic revival, and so on. Pigeonholing this chameleon-like practical academic is neither possible nor desirable. As he himself put it:

'I am like the cuckoo who lays her eggs in other birds' nests – the main thing is that the eggs should develop, not that the cuckoo's ego should be gratified.'

For the purpose of this essay, however, it is his overlapping roles as geographer and educator that are discussed.

Geddes's conception of geography stemmed from his evolutionary biological outlook; it was organic, it saw no major clash between the human and natural sciences. It was a geography mainly derived from his intellectual home, France, with its characteristic school of regional geography; and it was a geography that would appear in varied guises as 'sociology', 'civics', or 'geotechnics' because it offered him a multidisciplinary vehicle. Geddes gradually saw geography as 'the only complete science – the synthesis as the mother of them all'.

Equally generalist were his views on education and, however one labels him, Geddes was primarily an educator. Critical of schools and universities, he never lost an opportunity to proclaim his wide-ranging educational ideas. Take, for example, this extract from his letter of 1885 about his god-daughter and later co-worker, Mabel Barker:

'but I will heartily promise to stick by the wee lassie to the utmost of my power in so far as you entrust her education to me, to do my best for it. Suppose we begin at once, by suggesting for her earliest playthings as soon as she is old enough to handle things some pretty stones and shells from the beach... flowers too of course, and before she is two years old to be presented with a chunk of not too wet clay (Horror shrieks Mamma perhaps?) (No I don't think so after all) to make mud pies and to begin the practice of *solid* thoughts. I am not joking. A philosopher of my acquaintance is doing that with much effect upon his bairns'.

Such sentiments resonate with his belief:

'that the child's desire of seeing, touching, handling, smelling, tasting, and hearing are all true and healthy hungers, and these should be cultivated'.

Educating young Mabel about her environment was the most important aim of a 'true' education. Similar ideas characterise his planning philosophy: *Cities in Evolution* (1915) effectively spread his innovatory message that the key to dynamic social and urban improvement lay with an educated citizenry; Geddes's role was to teach them to see for themselves, to learn for themselves and to act on their own initiative. Awareness and participation were essential to the Geddes's ideas of citizenship.

Geography and his educational ideals, therefore, underpin many of Geddes's undertakings. Stemming from his eclectic interests came the concept of the regional survey. Arguably, regional survey was his main contribution to geography and education, and it was well described as 'the stock taking' of an area, an essential preliminary to effective, participatory planning. This essay develops Geddes's conception of regional survey, paying attention to its origins, its main characteristics, and the role of selected 'disciples', not just at university level but also in schools, in diffusing his message. Not only were these educators able and essential interpreters of the 'Gospel according to Geddes', but they were vigorous popularisers, who, critically but constructively, directly and indirectly, adapted his concepts to their own contexts and time.

Origins of Regional Survey

Biographers accept that his upbringing on Kinnoull Hill, overlooking Perth and the River Tay (Plate 5b), played a significant part in determining his world view. Here, he was introduced to gardening and nature study by his father, a recently retired Black Watch officer. Here, the commanding overview from Kinnoull's summit north to Strathmore and the Grampians, east to the Carse of Gowrie, and west to Strathearn and beyond, encouraged many rural rambles, with his father or like-minded friends, and further stimulated his curiosity. Environmental excursions such as these allowed him to collect botanical and geological specimens, to be examined and stored in the home-made 'laboratory' built by his father. And, although he was to reject many of its tenets, it was here in his home, Mount Tabor Cottage (Plate 5a), that his parents, devout Free Kirk members, might have introduced him to his favourite Old Testament Book – *Nehemiah* – with its post-exilic description of the rebuilding of Jerusalem's walls, perhaps his earliest initiation into the notion of urban renewal.

Further, it was from Kinnoull Hill that, from the age of eight, he daily journeyed across Smeaton's bridge to Perth Academy, then located in Rose Terrace, the elegant core of Georgian Perth overlooking the North Inch (Plate 6a). A particularly useful picture of Geddes's formal education is found in his 'Memories and Reflections'. Written at Montpellier, this article appeared in the 1928 *Young Barbarian*, the Perth Academy school magazine.

Contrary to expectation, the overall picture of education depicted by a reflective Geddes is a favourable one, and remarkably conformist. That he 'soon tired of Latin' scarcely distinguishes him from countless others; rather he admits to a good grounding in subjects such as English, French, Chemistry and, especially, Maths – a subject very well taught and 'made more real' by 'outdoor mensuration of heights and distances'. Significantly, he emphasised that Geometry was a life-long source of inspiration. This is reflected in his famous 'thinking machines', which allowed him in later years to demonstrate – to his (though not to everyone's) satisfaction – the interrelationships of different academic disciplines.

Thus, Geddes's upbringing on Kinnoull Hill shaped his formative years. It allowed him to experience the symbiotic relationships existing in nature, and to form his concept of the city and the region, from which there later emerged two significant explanatory devices at the heart of Regional Survey: the Outlook Tower and the Valley Section.

Regional Survey and Education: The Outlook Tower

It was in 1892 that Geddes (part-time Professor of Botany, from 1889, at University College, Dundee) acquired the Outlook Tower in Edinburgh's Castlehill, a significant vantage point on the crag-and-tail formation, the site for the historic Old Town. Geddes with his wife, Anna, had been deeply involved in slum redevelopment, the initiation of his Summer Schools, the establishment of the first student-run residences, and the building of Ramsay Garden; now he envisaged the Outlook Tower:

'as a place of outlook and as a type-museum which would serve not only as a key to a better understanding of Edinburgh and its region, but as a help towards the formation of clearer ideas of the city's relation to the world at large'.

Educationally, it was a multifunctional building: to assist the 'understanding' of the geographer, the historian, the sociologist, the artist and the social worker. In other words, it was a centre for civic and regional survey. Along with Riddle's Court, the Tower was used to host his Summer Schools.

Visitors followed Geddes to the top

'at break-neck speed. When they emerged on the narrow balcony around the turret they would be gasping for breath, and he claimed that they experienced the sudden panoramic views more intensely when the blood was circulating rapidly through their bodies'.

The rapid ascent was followed by 'guided' lectures from the polymathic Geddes on Edinburgh's townscapes in their regional context from the tower gallery, and in the darkness of the Camera Obscura. Afterwards Geddes would lead a 'concentric' descent of the Tower's five storeys, each appropriately furnished with varied graphic representations and equipment. First, the Edinburgh room housed relief models, maps, paintings and displays of the city's expansion (see Fig 4). The next storey was devoted to Scotland, emphasising the way in

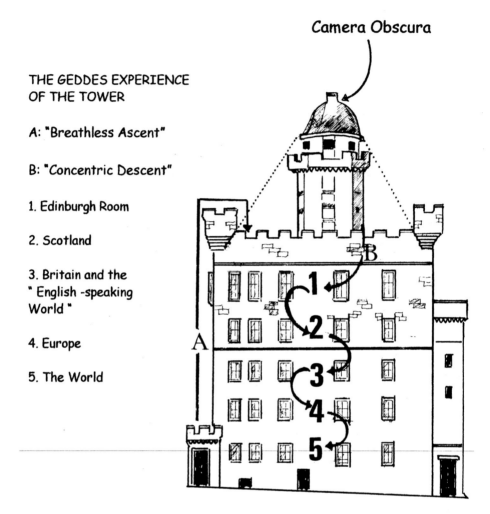

Camera Obscura

THE GEDDES EXPERIENCE
OF THE TOWER

A: "Breathless Ascent"

B: "Concentric Descent"

1. Edinburgh Room

2. Scotland

3. Britain and the
" English -speaking
World "

4. Europe

5. The World

Fig 13 The Geddes Experience of the Outlook Tower.
The Tower was reconstructed in 1852 as Short's Observatory when the camera obscura
was installed. The rebuilt lower floors survive from early 17th century tenements.
(Norman Thomson)

which geographical conditions had affected the country's history; the third
covered Britain and the English-speaking world, including the Empire and the
USA. Fourth came Europe; and then a final descent to the world room with its
displays of general anthropology and two large globes of relief and vegetation.
From 1895 to 1914 the Tower's displays were at their best, with Geddes frequently there as their expositor. Displays were altered according to his current
interests. Thus, when Theodore Zueblin visited the Tower – dubbed by him as
the 'World's First Sociological Laboratory' – the Europe floor displayed

material relating to Cyprus, recently visited by Geddes and his wife. (Anxious to assist Armenian refugees, who had fled Turkish oppression, Geddes produced a programme of land rejuvenation and small-scale agricultural schemes).

Overall, the layout and organisation of the Outlook Tower reflects Geddes's geographical and educational ideals. First, it demonstrated a concentric approach to geography, leading from the local to regional to national to the global; showing thereby 'Edinburgh's position within the vast scale of the universe' in a hierarchical fashion; as Murdo Macdonald has effectively phrased it:

'Every physical step on the way down the Tower... was also a cognitive step towards the integration of the local and the national'. It articulated with his former teacher TH Huxley's insistence on starting with the immediate environment, exemplified in his famous *Physiography* which begins with a study of the Thames.

Second, it played a significant role in his key objective of teaching people about their environment with its emphasis on civic knowledge and understanding. By improving environmental education a transformed environmental quality would ensue thanks to popular involvement in decision making.

Third, Edinburgh's Outlook Tower, and related 'Nature Palaces' or 'Geographical Museums' in the many plans that he made for towns and cities, were to function as vehicles of visual education. Maps, photographs, paintings, diagrams and panoramas – all were grist to his mill of visual thinking that blended art and science, and formed an integral part of his educational approach to regional survey.

Had his Dunfermline Report been realised, for example, the proposed 'Nature Institute' would have housed a series of panoramas, and its curator was to be 'one of those geographical artists' who would 'go to work upon a series of subjects carefully chosen with the help of a geographical committee... The series should naturally be arranged running north to south... The visitor... would begin, say with Nansen's sea of ancient ice, pass into Lapland with its Lapps and reindeer; descend to the pine forest of Norway with its sturdy woodman, its boat builder on the fiord, thence through Denmark or north Germany; a panel, therefore, depicting a North European Valley Section, taking the Dunfermline citizenry beyond their town to a global perspective'.

Regional Survey and Regional Education: The Valley Section

Another, related, visual teaching tool was the Valley Section, estimated by Geddes and his close collaborator, the sociologist Victor Branford, as 'the elemental diagram of regional survey'. A stained glass version of this apparently simple diagram appeared in the upper window of the Outlook Tower (see Plate x)

Fig 14 The Valley Section (Le Play Society Version)

'These are the tools which are needed by an explorer in your place, or any other:-
Ordnance Survey maps; camera; pocket lens; compass; knife and string; pencil and
pocket book; coloured pencils, inks or paints; tracing paper; a measuring tape is
also useful but, if you cannot get all these at first, begin with a note-book and pencil.'
(*Exploration: Regional Survey*, Le Play Society, ed. Mabel Barker, c 1933)

and is critically examined in detail by Murdo Macdonald. In various degrees of
complexity, the Valley Section was replicated in many publications on Regional
Survey by Geddes and his disciples. In his words it was 'that general slope from
mountain to sea which we find anywhere in the world' .

This particular version is taken from the Le Play Society publication
'Exploration: Regional Survey' ('Get to know your own Place and Work and
Folk'). This was edited by Geddes's god-daughter Mabel Barker mentioned
earlier. Ancient Scouts will notice a strong family resemblance to the section
on the Explorer's badge in the *Boy Scout's Handbook* of their youth.

Basically, the slope was a long profile of a river valley peopled by a variety
of 'occupational types'; hunters, miners, lumbermen, foresters and shepherds
in the uplands giving way to the farmers of the lowland, and the fishermen at
the coast. Also, where the valley broadens, there is the town or city at the
head of an estuary or at a strategic bridging point. Each urban settlement has
its own section of occupational types,

'which in their urban disguises, make up its population and impart to it
those characteristics which distinguish it from other towns'.

Essentially the Valley Section is an evolutionary diagram, a visual *longue
durée* in the terminology of the Annales school of history. Through time, the
farmer became the baker, the hunters furriers, the shepherd the wool mill
worker, and the miner the steel worker; stressing thereby in biological terms
the interdependence of the city or organism, and its region or habitat.

For Geddes, the Valley Section was a particularly useful model. There was a danger that such a device linking physical environment and economic life would be interpreted by some as inevitable, but Geddes saw the Valley Section as a model of social geography characterised by an ongoing struggle between people and their environment evolving through time: 'man must and can change his environment to suit his needs'. Educationally, the Valley Section was an excellent tool, serving not only regional survey but as a potential framework for the teaching of other subjects, such as arithmetic, as suggested in one of his surviving sheafs of notes, along with an outline part of a programme of geography teaching.

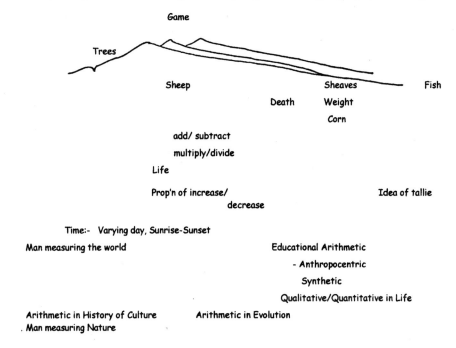

Fig 15 The Valley Section and Mathematics

The Valley Section as a framework for teaching maths, based on one of Geddes's files in the National Library of Scotland (NLS10619). (Norman Thomson).

With Fig 15 we feel as if we were looking over the great man's shoulder as he jots down his thoughts on the Valley Section as a framework for teaching Mathematics. This could be interpreted as an early example of the integrated day in the primary school.

In the last analysis, the Geddesian philosophy of education was summed up by his motto of *Vivendo Discimus* (By living we learn), which ideally involved merging the conventional book-based approach with a sampling of the varied occupational opportunities afforded along the Valley Section; and was perhaps best seen in the education of his eldest son Alasdair who among a variety of pursuits, beginning with assisting his father in the garden, herded sheep for a season, was cook on a herring boat... worked as a mason, and learned practical agriculture.

Regional Survey and Education: Continental Influences

The Outlook Tower and the Valley Section, therefore, are pivotal in Geddes's thinking about Regional Survey. That they were so significant stems from his formative years on Kinnoull, and, particularly, the later influence of French scholarship, and his admiration of the French peasantry. Geddes, via Edmond Demolins, derived from the mining engineer Frederic Le Play the notion that the key determinates of social structure were: *Lieu, Travail et Famille* or Place, Work and Family, the last of which Geddes widened to Folk (and which now in schools would be referred to as People). This triad of 'place/work/folk' was a counterpoint to his biological trilogy of environment/ function/organism. By demonstrating them in expanded form as Geography, Economics and Anthropology in multiple combinations on the squared paper of his 'thinking machines', Geddes set out

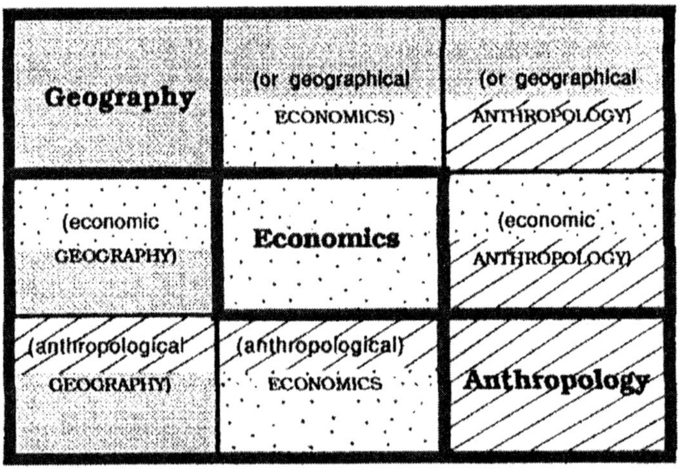

Geography	(or geographical ECONOMICS)	(or geographical ANTHROPOLOGY)
(economic GEOGRAPHY)	Economics	(economic ANTHROPOLOGY)
(anthropological GEOGRAPHY)	(anthropological) ECONOMICS	Anthropology

Fig 16 A Thinking Machine derived from 'Place, Work and Folk'.
The original triad has been adapted to take account of the social science disciplines – Geography, Economics and Anthropology. (Kenneth Maclean)

'his large-scale view of the relationship between the original formula of Le Play and the civic goal to which he aspired'.

Further enhancing his concept of Regional Survey, notably his Valley Section,

was the *Geographie Universelle* of Elisée Reclus, the French anarchist geographer. From his anarchist philosophy came visions of world brotherhood and harmony with Nature that helped to shape Geddes's conceptions of community and region. Stimulation also came from Reclus's fellow anarchist, the Russian geographer Pytor Kropotkin, who rejected the competitive dogma of social Darwinism in favour of co-operation. His *Fields, Factories and Workshop* (1888), influenced Geddes's ideas on regional interconnectedness. Overall, Geddes drank deeply at the well of the French School of geography; a geography that was more humanistic, more historical and less environmentally deterministic than any other. It was a geography rooted in what was still a basically rural country, with its distinctive *pays*, but whose methodology Geddes adapted to a highly urbanised Britain.

Reclus and Kropotkin not only communicated with Geddes, they were among the many participants in his Edinburgh Summer Schools. Scholars representing a range of disciplines gave lectures on a variety of themes; visits were conducted to sites such as the Pentland Hills, the historic burgh of Haddington, the newly opened Edinburgh Zoo, and along the shoreline at Port Seton; while the day concluded with programmes of cultural activities. Visiting lecturers included geographers and ecologists such as Edmond Demolins, Kropotkin, the Reclus brothers, Elie and Elisée, AJ Herbertson, GG Chisholm, M Newbigin and Ernst Haeckel, while educationists included CC Fagg and SS Laurie, Professor of Education at Edinburgh University, and his successor Alexander Darroch.

One of Laurie's interests centred on the life and work of the Czech-Moravian educationalist John Amos Comenius (1592-1670). Geddes highly esteemed the work of Comenius with whom, as Murdo Macdonald has stressed, he shared a common interest in a generalist educational outlook bridging science and the humanities, and a regard for nature as a field of study. Both educators emphasised the visual: Comenius's *Orbis Sensualis Pictus* (Visible World), whose first edition appeared in 1657, was illustrated by a series of wood-engravings of commonplace objects such as landscape features accompanied by short descriptions. Not only was it one of the earliest illustrated textbooks, including possibly the earliest urban model, but 'for some time it was the most popular textbook in Europe, and deservedly so'.

In the hands of Geddes, the presentation of the methods and results of Regional Survey was highly visual; as Mumford put it:

'if audio-visual methods of teaching have never been entirely lacking in schools since John Amos Comenius presented to teachers his *Orbis Sensualis Pictus*, the current enlargement of these methods owes not a little, at least in Britain, to Geddes' original initiatives'.

(250)

CXXIII.

The inward parts   *Interiora Urbis,*
of a City.

Within a City	**Intra Urbem**
are Streets, 1.	sunt *Plateæ* (Vici) 1.
paved with Stones :	lapidibus stratæ :
Market-places, 2.	*Fora,* 2.
(in some places	(alicubi
with Galleries) 3.	cum *Porticibus*) 3.
and narrow Lanes, 4.	& *Angiportus.* 4.
The publick buildings	Publica ædificia sunt
are in the middle of the	in medio Urbis,
the Church, 5. (City,	*Templum,* 5.
the School, 6.	*Schola,* 6.
the Guild-hall, 7.	*Curia,* 7.
the Exchange. 8.	*Domus Mercatura* : 8.
	About

(251)

About the walls,	Circa Mænia,
and the Gates,	& Portas,
are the Magazine, 9	*Armamentarium,* 9.
the Granary, 10.	*Granarium,* 10.
Innes,	*Diverforia,*
Ale-houfes,	*Popinæ,*
Cooks-shops, 11	& *Caupanæ,* 11.
the Play-houfe, 12.	*Theatrum,* 12.
and the Spittle ; 13.	*Nofodochium* ; 13.
In the by-places	In receffibus,
are houses of office,14.	*Forica* (Cloacæ) 14.
and the Prifon. 15.	& *Cuftodia*(Carcer)15.
In the chief Steeple	In Turre primariâ
is the Clock, 16.	eft *Horologium,* 16.
and the Watchmens	& habitacio
dwelling. 17.	*Vigilum.* 17.
In the Streets	In Plateis
are Wells. 18.	funt *Putei.* 18.
The River 19.	*Fluvius,* 19.
a Beck	vel *Rivus,*
runing about the City,	Urbem interfluens,
ferveth	infervit
to wafh away the filth.	*fordibus* eluendis.
The Tower 10.	*Arx* 20.
ftandeth in the higheft	exftat
part of the City.	in fummo Urbis.

Judge-

Fig. 17 The 'Urban Model' of Comenius
One of the many woodcut sketches from his *Orbis Sensualium Pictus. (Woburn Press)*

Regional Survey and Education: University Geographers Spread the Gospel

From the late 1880s, Geddes had agitated for Regional Survey as a key part of his educational credo as well as playing an active role in planning. To Geddes, Regional Survey was a purposeful, robust mechanism – not 'a mundane and dull thing but a tool for a new age'. As expressed in his *Cities in Evolution*:

'Regional Survey and its applications – Rural Development, Town Planning, City Design – these are destined to become master-thoughts and practical ambitions for the opening generation'.

Yet credit for the diffusion of his views and the creation of the Geddesian tradition 'for a new age' mainly lies with geographers, planners and teachers, particularly in the inter-war period. Attention now turns to sample Geddesian protagonists of Regional Survey: firstly, at university level in Britain; and secondly, in schools.

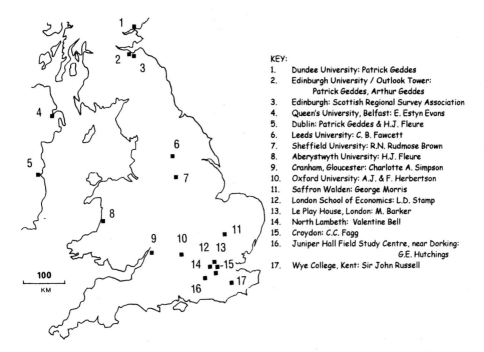

KEY:
1. Dundee University: Patrick Geddes
2. Edinburgh University / Outlook Tower:
   Patrick Geddes, Arthur Geddes
3. Edinburgh: Scottish Regional Survey Association
4. Queen's University, Belfast: E. Estyn Evans
5. Dublin: Patrick Geddes & H.J. Fleure
6. Leeds University: C. B. Fawcett
7. Sheffield University: R.N. Rudmose Brown
8. Aberystwyth University: H.J. Fleure
9. Cranham, Gloucester: Charlotte A. Simpson
10. Oxford University: A.J. & F. Herbertson
11. Saffron Walden: George Morris
12. London School of Economics: L.D. Stamp
13. Le Play House, London: M. Barker
14. North Lambeth: Valentine Bell
15. Croydon: C.C. Fagg
16. Juniper Hall Field Study Centre, near Dorking:
    G.E. Hutchings
17. Wye College, Kent: Sir John Russell

Fig. 18 Spreading the Gospel according to Geddes

Summer schools conducted by academics influenced, directly or indirectly, by
Geddes in the period 1890-1930. *(Norman Thomson)*

Fig 18 shows some of the universities and individuals who, in their research,
writings and teaching disseminated Geddes's ideas. Three individuals may be
cited by way of illustration. At Edinburgh University was Dr Arthur Geddes
(1895-1968), the second son, and who, from 1927 onwards, taught courses
on social, historical and regional geography, particularly South Asia. The central
themes of 'place/work/folk' influenced much of his work, not least in his writings
on South Asia, especially India where, at his father's request, he was first in
residence from 1921 to 24. This brought him into contact with one of his father's
main correspondents – the Indian poet, philosopher, mystic and educator
Rabindranath Tagore (1861-1941), who had founded a school at Shantiniketan,
from which base the poet started on his next educational project – the
International University, Visva-Bharati. During his stay, Arthur immersed himself in the place. He learned Bengali, worked in rural construction projects, participated in cultural events, and researched the landscapes and peoples of
Bengal, resulting in his postgraduate thesis '*Au pays de Tagore*'.

Arthur Geddes's reputation for his work on India, including studies of
population and medical geography, earned for him the apposite comment that his

'model of landscape geography'... maintained 'the dialectic between scientific abstraction and the observable world, the one we can see, hear, smell and touch', an endorsement of which his demanding father would have approved. Nor did he neglect Scotland: there were historical geographical studies of its small towns and villages and changing rural landscapes.

William Hesketh Lever (Lord Leverhulme) created an industrial empire from soap which, with abundant pure water from the great Victorian dams and reservoirs, brought about a revolution in public health. He created Port Sunlight as an Utopia for his workers, and it retains its charm after a century. He set up a splendid art gallery with free access and founded a Department of Civic Design at the University of Liverpool. The war memorial to all the Unilever workers who served and died in World War 1 is centrally situated where all can remember them. In 1917 he bought Lewis for £143,000 and set about transforming the island, based on a modern fishing industry. But the Lewismen returning from the war wanted only land and would not co-operate. Lever gave them a park in Stornoway and sold them back their compulsorily purchased houses at a loss – and moved his operation to Harris, which he bought in 1919. At Ob, renamed Leverburgh in the best eighteenth century entrepreneurial tradition, his ships and factories flourished, leading to Mac Fisheries, Bird's Eye, PG Tips, Hellmann's Mayonnaise and Pot Noodle. But not in Harris, Lever's death in 1925 taking the edge off that enterprise.

Patrick Geddes and Leverhulme knew of each other's activities and clearly had some parallel objectives. In the summer of 1914 Geddes's Cities Exhibition was in Dublin. One Sunday afternoon the only person in charge was Lady Aberdeen, the Vicereine, when the slum-dwellers of Dublin looted the Exhibition. Leverhulme was delighted that his model of Port Sunlight had disappeared, seeing this as the greatest compliment he could have received –

'Each thief would have a model of a little cottage on his mantelpiece and that would show him the sort of place he should be living in, instead of in the slums.'

What a tragedy that Geddes and he did not work together! With Lever's wealth and directed energy he would have been a splendid patron, for whom Geddes's humanity could have generated real changes in society. Arthur, however, was involved. He first visited Lewis in 1919 as assistant to the French biogeographer and fellow Geddesian, Marcel Hardy, surveying the island for the disparagingly-nicknamed (by the proud islanders) 'Soapman' and later did wartime work there for the Department of Health. Assessed by a former student as a 'brilliant and inspiring teacher, particularly with a small tutorial or seminar group' (though 'the shadow of Sir Patrick seemed to be over-prevalent'), Dr Geddes's approach reflected his gallimaufry of interests that were possibly too wide for the focussed lecture, and for less tolerant students only seeking examination success.

By the early 'sixties at Edinburgh University, Arthur's teaching load was confined to his Regional Monsoon Asia course and a Friday afternoon seminar on the Philosophy of Geography. On one of these occasions, after the usual display of pyrotechnics interlaced with obscurity, Arthur concluded the working week by summing up:

'Remember, just remember, if you have any creative notion, the slightest spark of an idea, water it well and let it grow!'

Another Geddesian, whose geography was equally wide-ranging, was Guernsey-born Herbert John Fleure (1876-1969). Trained like PG in the natural sciences, Fleure switched to physical anthropology and geography, and was appointed to the chair of Geography and Anthropology at Aberystwyth in 1917. This was the first British university to establish an honours degree course in geography in both arts and science, and this at a time when geography was scarcely accepted as a university discipline. A tribute to Fleure's holistic educational and geographical philosophy: it was 'the special duty and privilege of Geography to serve as a link between the two faculties'.

Fleure had collaborated with Geddes at the 1914 Cities and Town Planning Exhibition in Dublin and, throughout his career, 'the sparkling mind of Sir Patrick Geddes' was highly influential. In many respects Fleure is seen as the most enthusiastic of his geographical interpreters; but, although his evolutionary and regional perspectives matched those of Geddes, he differed, for example, with regard to the Valley Section. To Fleure, it savoured too much of determinism, neglected watersheds as possible sites for settlement, and equated the concept of the region with a river basin.

Instead, he re-worked Geddesian concepts of society and environment, often with insights from archaeology and anthropology, into a more dynamic form, that came 'closer to the Geddesian ideal of humanistic synthesis than Geddes ever did'. Perhaps this is best seen in his famous paper on 'Human Regions' in which he discussed regions of difficulty, of privation, of debilitation, of increment, of industrialisation, of nomadism. None of these regions was unchanging in character; change stemmed not only from an evolutionary dialectic between place and people, but more significantly between people and people, as seen, for example, in Darfur province, Sudan, today. Although this was a stimulating paper demonstrating his geographical breadth, its impact was lessened by the absence of maps delimiting his regions; or as Livingstone more aptly puts it: Fleure's 'humanised regionalism could not traffic in cartographic precision'.

Regardless of differences of interpretation that existed between the two men, there is no doubt that Geddes

'clearly provided Fleure with constant inspiration, and... despite a more sophisticated articulation of ideas he never deviated from the basic postulates of the Geddesian framework... and rendered them accessible and acceptable to geography'.

Apart from his teaching at Aberystwyth and, from 1930 to 44, at Manchester

University, Fleure was able to further the development of geography when he succeeded AJ Herbertson as Honorary Secretary of the Geographical Association, and later, as Honorary Editor. Articles and reviews in the Association's *The Geographical Teacher*, renamed *Geography* in 1925, and contributions to other leading journals, testify to the power and persuasiveness of Fleure's pen at a significant time in the advancement of Regional Survey and other geographical issues.

It was in the pages of *The Geographical Teacher* for 1915 that the shrewd observation was made:

'Nine out of every ten who have known Herbertson will remember him... for his great efforts in connection with geographical education rather than geographical science'.

The obituarist – Sir Halford Mackinder (1861-1947), geographer, geopolitician and educationalist – had been appointed Reader in Geography at Oxford University in 1887. The deceased, AJ Herbertson (1865-1915) had been persuaded in 1899 by Mackinder to join him in the first British university department of geography as his assistant, significantly with the title of Lecturer in Regional Geography. When Mackinder left Oxford in 1905, Herbertson became head of department, and was given a personal chair in 1910.

Born in Galashiels, Herbertson had trained in the physical sciences, particularly physics, at Edinburgh University. Later studies were undertaken at varying times at Freiburg, Paris and Montpellier, where he was initiated into the study of plant geography. Meteorological research was conducted by him at the Ben Nevis Observatory. As Demonstrator in Botany he assisted Patrick Geddes in Dundee; and his teaching career as a geographer began in Manchester University in 1894, and at the Heriot Watt College two years later. His was a long and varied apprenticeship, but he was rewarded in 1898 with his PhD from Freiburg on 'The monthly distribution of rainfall over the world'. Such research interests in global climatic phenomena, coupled with work on plant associations, led to his concept of using major natural regions as an aid to teaching.

Although his 1904 original paper – 'The Major Natural Regions' – was not well received by the fellows at the Royal Geographical Society, it was a marked advance in geographical education; in the words of L Dudley Stamp:

'It would be difficult to cite any other single communication which has had such far reaching effects in the development of our subject.'

Difficult for us to understand, however, is that it was only a century ago that we had this first proper systematic statement of how our planet is divided up, instead of vague generalisations. Partly derived from Geddesian regionalism, Herbertson's approach offered teachers an alternative framework to the prevailing country-by-country review of physical features and products. In a later elaboration, Herbertson suggested that:

'Not merely is time saved, but a more accurate knowledge of the world is

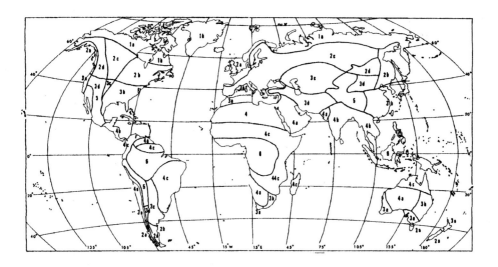

1. Polar (a) Lowlands (Tundra type)
   (b) Highlands (Ice-cap type)
2. The cool temperate regions
   (a) Western margin (West European type)
   (b) Eastern margin (Quebec type)
   (c) Interior lowlands (Siberian type)
   (d) Interior mountain area (Altai type)
3. The warm temperate regions
   (a) Western margin with winter rains
    (Mediterranean type)
   (b) The eastern margin with summer
    rains (China type)
   (c) The interior lowlands (Turan type)
   (d) and the plateau (Iran type)

4. (a) The west tropical deserts (Sahara type)
  (b) East tropical lands (Monsoon type)
  (c) Inter-tropical tablelands (Sudan type)
5. Lofty tropical or sub-tropical mountains
 (Tibetan type)
6. Equatorial lowlands (Amazon type)

Fig. 19 AJ Herbertson's map of the world, classified into natural regions.

(Kenneth Maclean)

gained, the memory is not burdened by a plethora of place names... For him the world becomes real and the names learned recall real scenes. He is compelled to make comparisons and seek out reasons for likenesses and differences. Geography ceases to be a mere memory subject'.

It was a remarkably successful approach: numerous textbooks illustrating 'place/work/folk' were written by him, often in collaboration with his wife, Dorothy. Over 1.4 million textbooks came from the Clarendon Press, one of them – *Man and his Work* – appearing in eight editions between 1899 and 1963 – an interesting comment on both the quality of the book and the conservatism of teachers.

Arthur Geddes, HJ Fleure and AJ Herbertson, therefore, are just a sample of Geddesian protagonists who, to use Mumford's term, followed the 'Master'. In spreading the Geddesian credo, there were certain common features.

Early departments of geography essentially functioned as nurseries, rearing the future lecturers and school teachers. Considerable stress was laid, therefore, on the teaching of regional geography. For example, Fleure's teaching syllabus at Aberystwyth in the 1920s

'bore the unquestionable imprint of Herbertson's influence... Of the five theory papers, four were entirely regional... and were entitled – The Regional Geography of the British Isles; the Regional Geography of Europe; the Regional Geography of the Southern Continents; and the Regional Geography of the Lands of the Romance Languages.'

Likewise, at Edinburgh University, Professor AG Ogilvie – Herbertson's assistant from 1912 to 1914 – saw regional geography for his Honours students 'as the culmination of the course, with the full use of topographical maps and visual aids'.

Fieldwork was stressed as an integral part of departmental syllabi. For example, two former Departmental Heads of Geography/Social Studies at Moray House College of Education, recall Dr Arthur Geddes leading Junior Honours students at Edinburgh University into houses in Edinburgh's Royal Mile and conducting 'folk' surveys in the early 1950s. Fieldwork was encouraged by the Le Play Society. Established in 1930, under the presidency of Geddes, it was strongly promoted by his followers, and over the next thirty years many geographers took part in over eighty excursions, mainly in Europe but also in the British Isles.

Geographers such as Arthur Geddes (Eastern Pyrenees), Herbert J Fleure (Eastern Carpathians) and L Dudley Stamp (Finland and Slovenia) both taught and learned about 'place/work/folk' in rural contexts, fostering regional survey methods, and producing a series of monographs and articles. Such surveys have been criticised as too wide-ranging and descriptive, and emphasising rural environments at the expense of urban – 'middle-aged schoolmarms prying into peasant cottages'. But survey methodologies are flexible, and, by the early 1960s, no fewer than 'two professors-emeriti and nine present holders of geography chairs' had led many students and teachers on Le Play Society excursions.

Large numbers of students and teachers attended Summer Schools organised by universities such as Aberystwyth and Oxford. Over 850 students, predominantly teachers, attended the five biennial Summer Schools at Oxford organised by Herbertson and his wife, between 1906 and 1914. A keen advocate of Summer Schools, Herbertson had served his apprenticeship under Geddes, assisting at the Outlook Tower; a 'symbiotic relationship' as Meller phrases it:

'Herbertson, practical, conscientious and hard working, and Geddes mercurial, bubbling with ideas, but lacking the patience for practical application.'

Over the years, distinguished geographers, including the geomorphologist WM Davies, JF Unstead and RN Rudmose Brown contributed to busy programmes of field excursions and lectures. In 1910, over 250 attended and had the opportunity to listen to Patrick Geddes on 'Cities'. Part of a series of lectures

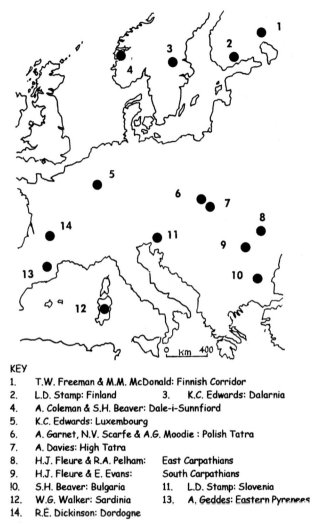

KEY
1. T.W. Freeman & M.M. McDonald: Finnish Corridor
2. L.D. Stamp: Finland   3.   K.C. Edwards: Dalarnia
4. A. Coleman & S.H. Beaver: Dale-i-Sunnfiord
5. K.C. Edwards: Luxembourg
6. A. Garnet, N.V. Scarfe & A.G. Moodie : Polish Tatra
7. A. Davies: High Tatra
8. H.J. Fleure & R.A. Pelham: East Carpathians
9. H.J. Fleure & E. Evans: South Carpathians
10. S.H. Beaver: Bulgaria   11.   L.D. Stamp: Slovenia
12. W.G. Walker: Sardinia   13.   A. Geddes: Eastern Pyrenees
14. R.E. Dickinson: Dordogne

Fig. 20 Sample Excursions conducted by the Le Play Society; 1920s-1950s.
(Norman Thomson)

on the British Isles, his course is detailed in the *The Geographical Teacher* for 1910, and in three parts covers: 'The Geography of Cities'; 'The History of Cities'; and 'The Life of Cities'. Furthermore, a series of seminar questions are given, including:

'Colour town-plans to indicate the essential character of nineteenth century Oxford,

How would you plan out a survey of your town preparatory to the initiation of its town planning schemes?

How would you arrange your material for a local exhibition, such as might be held in the City Museum or Library, or at the Town hall?'

Commenting favourably on the course outline, urban geographer Brian Robson maintained that:

'Its blend of description, of sociological interpretation, of history, and of social roles, embodies in embryo much of the now-grown tissue of urban geography'.

In these ways and through his university 'disciples', Geddes's ideas were spread to a growing number of teachers at secondary and primary level. Key questions are: how did the rhetoric of Regional Survey translate into practice in the schools? Were all schools affected, and who were the Geddesians in the schools?

Regional Survey and Education: Spreading the Gospel in the Schools

The changes initiated by Geddes and his acolytes did not extinguish traditional teaching modes. Curricular innovation was, as Withers has stressed, a question of locality – 'where one studied geography determined what sorts of geography one was taught'. This partly stemmed from the fact that the 1912 *Memorandum on the teaching of geography in Scottish primary schools* was not prescriptive. Instead broad guidelines were laid down allowing varied interpretation. At secondary school, relatively few received a geographical education beyond the intermediate level, while in the Leaving Certificate, geography was grouped with English. Variations, therefore, existed in the provision of geographical education between schools; a situation further complicated by the adoption or rejection of innovatory measures associated with the methods of Regional Survey. Some case studies now illustrate the period from the 1890s to the 1970s.

School Excursions in the Dunfermline Area

Although Dunfermline is associated with Patrick Geddes and his famous 1904 planning report for the Carnegie Dunfermline Trust, the Fife town had already attracted his attention. Addressing the first meeting of the Dunfermline Naturalists' Society in 1902, he suggested that: 'Nature-interest, Nature-lore, Nature-literature are all coming into place', and Dunfermline citizens of all ages could benefit from excursions in the Forth valley:

'Returning from our regional excursions, we shall see more interest in the familiar city ...and interpret not only its present but its past, its possibilities in the future also.'

Such thoughts were not new to those familiar with his ideas, but they were now reinforced by a successful series of experimental field excursions conducted over a four year period from 1897. Instigated by Geddes, they were financed for the first three years by his friend, Henry Beveridge of Pitreavie, a local philanthropist who had resigned from the family business – St Leonard's Linen Works – to pursue his interests in natural history and archaeology. Initially the excursions were organised on Saturdays, switching to schooldays once their value had been demonstrated to the school boards. They involved parties of Primary Six pupils in parties up to thirty, with 'at least two teachers... to preserve order and to gain experience in conducting such excursions'. Train and ferry took the parties to Stirling, Edinburgh, Perth, Inchcolm, Linlithgow, and sometimes included coastal walks, for example, between Kirkcaldy and Dysart. Geddes himself was not involved; instead, the excursions were led by TR Marr, AJ Herbertson and Robert Smith, whose maps of the Edinburgh district and North Perthshire initiated vegetation mapping of Scotland. Use was made of maps and compasses, and pupils were encouraged to observe, record and interpret the field evidence; field note books were kept and specimens were collected.

Comments like those above echoed other advocates of fieldwork in Scotland, among whom were progressive educationists such as Aberdeen University's Professor of Logic and early advocate of psychology, Alexander Bain, who recommended that it was

'necessary to take the class out of doors, in Saturday excursions, to mark with express attention the surrounding scenery... and to conceive the town or village as a whole... and... from some commanding eminence that a pupil should receive first impressions of Geography.'

There were scientists like the geologist Archibald Geikie, whose innovative book *The Teaching of Geography* (1887) also highlighted the advantages of local field study:

'It is hardly possible to overrate the benefit that arises from this co-operation of teacher and taught in the open air... directing their eyes to the outer world and leading them to take reverent heed of what may there be seen'.

Likewise, continental influences were significant. Geikie's ideas reflected in part the strength of *heimatskunde* (home study), and among a considerable number of early articles offering advice on fieldwork in *The Geographical Teacher*, was one on the German *Wandervogel* movement for youngsters – published in 1905, it must be said. The movement was:

'designed to awaken in them a taste for the beauties of nature... and opportunities of learning to know their German homeland and its people at first hand.'

The Dunfermline excursions should be seen, therefore, in a context of geographically dispersed, popular, local scientific societies promoting geographical and nature study programmes, and growing educational pressure for change. Thanks to vigorous campaigning on the part of Geddes and his collaborator J Arthur Thomson, Professor of Natural Science at Aberdeen University, Nature Study became part of the Scottish schools' curriculum in 1899, with England following a year later.

Norman Miller Johnson: 'Regional Survey and Education'

The success of Geography and Nature Study in schools depended in no small measure on the commitment and enthusiasm of teachers and their headteachers. The Autumn 1924 *The Geographical Teacher* carried an article entitled 'Regional Survey and Education'. Written by Norman M Johnson (1887-1949), Headmaster of Kinglassie Public School, Fife, it detailed Regional Survey work carried out in the school.

Pertinent comments are made by Johnson concerning constraints hindering the spread of Regional Survey methods:

'There is no doubt that in Scotland, at least, owing to examination conditions, such work in detail can be carried out only by supplementary pupils' (ie. those pupils, not selected for a Higher Grade school – Kirkcaldy High School in this instance – and who remained at school from 12 to 14). 'In the hands of a sympathetic teacher, however, there is no hindrance to the Regional attitude being adopted throughout. It may be a surprise to many teachers to know that Regional work is recommended in the Scottish Code.'

Johnson cites part of the 1915 Code recommending Regional Survey:

'many items worthy of record would occur to the thoughtful teacher... and... a school might even aim at building up its own *Book of Regional Survey...* a storehouse of valuable information concerning the locality.'

Such comments, therefore, reiterate the importance of dedication to Regional Survey on the part of teachers, and relate to Withers' emphasis on the unevenness of curricular innovation.

Norman J Johnson, doubtless, was a dedicated devotee of Regional Survey throughout his teaching career. Educated at Manchester University, he taught in Fife: first at Kirkcaldy High School teaching maths and science; then as headteacher at Kinglassie (1920-1924); and as headteacher in two Dunfermline Schools – McLean Public School (1924-1936), and Commercial School (1936-1942), when he retired. Examination of the school log books and his varied writings, as well as recollections by a former pupil, reveal strongly the influence of Geddes on Johnson in several ways.

(This is an appropriate point at which to remind the reader that headteachers in Scottish schools were required by law to keep a log book. These are obviously important historical sources, although their value varies according to the idiosyncrasies of successive headteachers. Johnson was not required to record his Geddesian exploits, he did so because he thought them important. It is one of the great mysteries that the headteacher at Castlehill School, in Edinburgh, seems not to have considered anything about Geddes worth recording. Yet his school lay between the Outlook Tower and the Geddes flat in Ramsay Garden. We know that pageants took place in the school and that the children marched down Castlehill to their new garden, led by Alasdair and the pipes.)

At Kinglassie, local fieldwork involved climbing the hill (605 feet/184 metres) immediately north of the village to a local tower (see Plate 6b) –

'a visit was made to Blythe's Tower – the school 'Outlook Tower', and the immediate school district was linked up with a considerable area of the Scottish Lowlands. All prominent points were identified, and each child drew an outline panorama.'

Diagrams were drawn as part of classroom display work. These showed:

'application of the 'Valley Section' to (a) immediate district, (b) wider district from West Lomond to Kinghorn.'

In the early 1920s such a Valley Section would have revealed 'occupational types' ranging from the miners in Kinglassie, hill shepherds in the Lomonds, farmers in the lowlands, and fishers and hoteliers along the coast.

Various nature study excursions were held during the year and the results discussed:

'7 Sep 1922. gave Nature Study lesson to Sen III (Autumn topics generally treated & migration of birds in some detail).

8 Nov. Taught N.S. to Supple. Gave N.S. lesson to Sen I and Sen II on fungi found during outdoor excursion'. (from the Kinglassie Public School Log 1917-1950).

Throughout his period as headteacher at Kinglassie, Johnson not only built up an impressive 'storehouse of valuable information', but he also conducted in-service courses:

'1923: 31 August New history pictures put up in certain classrooms, also OS maps of district. Regional Survey materials put up, also maps of Fife.

6 Sep. After school hours over 30 teachers from Auchterderran district visited the school. I demonstrated the Regional Survey Exhibition to them.'

Although not equating exactly with a Summer School atop Castlehill, such a course was no less significant in terms of its educational potential.

Museums and exhibitions were important.

'Feb 10, 1937 Headmaster choosing further museum specimens in Edinburgh for use of local schools.

13 June, 1938 Sixty children from Sen. I classes at Empire Exhibition'.

Held at Glasgow's Bellahouston Park, over a hundred pavilions displayed features of 'place/work/people' from the United Kingdom and most of the 'scattered members of the 'family' of the 'British Empire'. Such exhibitions had found favour with Geddes, not least because of their visual qualities. At the 1900 Paris Exhibition, he had let loose his own children

'and they went to these panoramas again and again, and in this way educated themselves by the eye'.

Significantly, the 1938-39 *Report on Commercial Public School* by His

Majesty's Inspector of Schools praised the pupils' co-operative exhibition project after the visit to Glasgow; the 'admirable initiative' in using 'graphical, pictorial and practically constructed aids'; and the fact that 'the staff is particularly strong on the scientific side, and nature study and geography are made specially interesting'. Former pupil Tom Masterton recalls quite vividly an impromptu lesson on water and ice by Johnson, triggered by a fellow pupil bringing a frozen milk bottle to school.

As part of the Geddesian ideal of the Nature Study movement, small gardens were cultivated by pupils, including Tom Masterton, at Commercial School in the pre-war period. Such an educational land use had been proposed in Geddes's Trial Garden, indicated in his Dunfermline Report. And, as suggested in the same report, the Glen in Pittencrieff Park was used by the Commercial School pupils for the study of rocks.

The HMI also singled out for praise the use of audio-visual methods. Not only was a special room set up for

'projection work... in connection with geography and nature study... but... these are linked up, where possible with broadcast talks.'

Johnson was an early pioneer in the use of broadcasts. At Kinglassie, on 23 April 1924:

'Due to the kindness of Mr and Mrs Bingham, the staff and pupils were able to 'listen in' to the opening ceremony at the British Empire Exhibition at Wembley.'

In the late 1930s, he was a member of the BBC geography sub-committee, among whose members was Professor AG Ogilvie of Edinburgh University. BBC geography broadcasts had started nationally on 16 January, 1925, with a series of 'Travel Talks' for younger pupils, produced by HJ Fleure, and by 1936/37 the Scottish Regional transmitters' programmes on 'The Empire Overseas' and 'The British Isles' were bringing case studies of 'place/work/people' into the class-room; a teaching situation assisted by well-illustrated booklets.

Furthermore, the log book for Commercial School shows that extensive use was being made of filmstrips, then superseding lantern slides. In fact, details in the log book listing the titles of filmstrips e.g. 'October 15, 1937 Film lessons' – 'Coalmining, Auvergne, Fife Industries' seem disproportionately to outweigh other 'normal' issues of absenteeism etc.

Johnson was a teacher with a Geddesian sense of priorities.

He also wrote extensively. From his pen came several textbooks; articles on biogeography e.g. in *Scottish Geographical Magazine* – 'A Method of mapping the distribution of Marine Algae'; and various articles in the Dunfermline Press: for example an 'Early Survey of Dunfermline'. But his magnum opus is a large A2 size, two hundred page, fully illustrated *Survey of Dunfermline and District* (1946) (Plate 7a). The proud librarian, Mrs Jeanette McMullen, displays this Dunfermline treasure. Written after his retiral in 1942, and before Johnson under-

Fig. 21 Front covers of two BBC Scotland Geography pamphlets.
Well-illustrated and informative sources for teachers and pupils.
(Kenneth Maclean)

took training for the Church of Scotland ministry, it is a detailed labour of love tracing Dunfermline's morphology; replete with maps, diagrams, press cuttings and commentaries, it is an exemplar *Book of Regional Survey.*

Dudley Stamp and the Land Utilisation Survey

In terms of scale of results and number of people involved the Land Utilisation Survey of Britain marked the high point of Regional Survey. It was no mean undertaking, and marked the first comprehensive survey of land use in the British Isles. From 1930 to 1934, the Survey was mainly carried out by two hundred and fifty thousand school children from some ten thousand schools, under the guidance of their geography teachers. The land use was recorded on the six-inch Ordnance Survey maps, with their field boundaries; a seven-fold classification was employed to categorise the land; and the results were collated and analysed at the London School of Economics, transferred to one-inch maps, and accompanying reports edited by Dudley Stamp, were published on a county basis.

Ultimately, the Land Use Survey was rooted in the work of the Regional Surveys Committee of the Geographical Association, whose secretary was L Dudley Stamp (1898-1966). A Londoner by birth, and a geologist and geographer by training, Stamp by 1930 was Reader in Economic Geography at the LSE. At a time of declining agricultural production, Stamp, a self-styled 'applied geographer' saw the need for a full scale national assessment of 'the utility and potential of each acre of British land'. Surveys such as those conducted by the Regional Surveys Committee were too piecemeal; and Stamp became not only a very effective director of the Land Use Survey, but generously steered the gravy train, with its operations mainly financed with royalties earned from his very considerable output of geography texts for schools, particularly *The World*, read by millions of school pupils throughout the Empire.

Dudley Stamp was a prolific writer, with over a hundred titles to his credit – although clever (and jealous) critics in the 'sixties said he had written one book a hundred times! This was simply not true, for example, he wrote *The Developing World* when others were still trying to cope with the concept of The Third World. He always had a few file cards in his breast pocket and at a social occasion it was comforting to know that one's wise remarks would appear soon in another Dudley Stamp book. One of the few geographers to have been on 'Desert Island Discs', his choice of luxury was an unlimited supply of paper and pencils!

By undertaking this mammoth task, Stamp maintained that the practical educational benefits of surveying and mapping would be matched by a training in citizenship, that

'would awaken an intelligent interest in the meaning and influence of environment, and so in the development of civic consciousness and local *esprit de corps*'.

When complete, the maps with their attractive covers, designed by the Ordnance Survey artist, Ellis Martin, were popular with a growing inter-war public increasingly keen on outdoor leisure pursuits, motoring and escaping the cities, and were frequently displayed in railway stations and estate agents' windows.

Additionally, the results of the survey were mobilised in the cause of wartime planning for increased domestic food production, and the creation of the 'New Jerusalem', notably in the work of the Scott Committee (1941-43) – one of several such bodies on which Stamp served – charged with examining the future of the countryside. By their espousal of such causes, Dudley Stamp and Patrick Geddes are united as examples of regional geographers and planners who believed that:

'by encouraging a sense of local and national citizenship based upon a holistic understanding of natural and social processes, regional survey would lead logically to planning'.

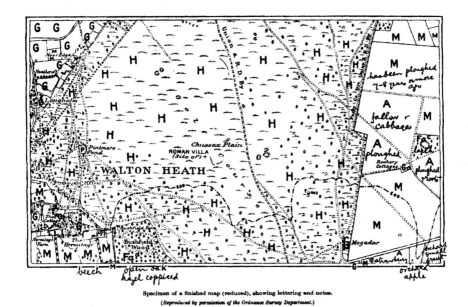

Specimen of a finished map (reduced), showing lettering and notes.
(Reproduced by permission of the Ordnance Survey Department.)

Fig. 22 Sample of early 1930s Land Utilisation Survey map.

Part of a quite unique educational achievement, that fully fulfilled Geddes's concept of geography. *(Kenneth Maclean)*

Tom Masterton and 'Environmental Studies: A Concentric Approach'

Fig 23 shows a simplified urban growth map suitable for primary school children, and is found in Tom Masterton's *Environmental Studies: A Concentric Approach* of 1969. This influential book was designed for primary teachers and trainee teachers in colleges of education, and is worth considering as a college lecturer's response to contemporary curricular thinking on environmental studies in Scotland. At the time of publication, its author was a Senior Lecturer in the Geography department of Moray House College of Education, now Edinburgh University's Faculty of Education.

Environmental Studies deals with five 'centres of interest', rather than adopting a more conventional disciplinary ('geography', 'history', 'science') approach. Beginning with Arthur's Seat, the author discusses the potential of such a hill for fieldwork, stressing that

'the child should not be asked to look in a specialised way at the landscape. Everything the child is interested in can be regarded as relevant. Also relevant are any disciplines which can contribute skills and techniques to aid the study of the whole landscape.'

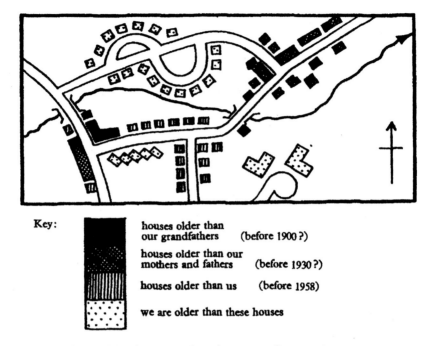

Key: houses older than
our grandfathers (before 1900 ?)

houses older than our
mothers and fathers (before 1930 ?)

houses older than us (before 1958)

we are older than these houses

FIGURE IV.3 A map to show how part of a town has grown

Fig. 23 Urban Growth map suitable for use in Primary Schools.
Housing classified by age. *(TH Masterton)*

From this local exemplar, the study moves outwards to distant mountainous areas, conforming to the concentric approach, about which we are reminded:

'Environmental work need not end with the study of *us, our* folk, in *our place, now.* This would be egocentric... Its ideas and techniques can be used to study *other folk in their place, now.*'

Furthermore, by using photographs, maps, models, statistics and 'vivid word descriptions', pupils observe, record and think about what they have seen. Such an approach underpins the remaining chapters covering food, water, houses and weather.

Reviewers were impressed, not least because a

'valuable lesson of this book is, that if one specialist in a particular discipline ...can successfully evolve a many-sided approach to Environmental Studies... then so ought the rest of us.'

Such a 'many-sided approach' stems from two factors. In the first place, the book was a response to the 1965 memorandum 'Primary Education in Scotland' (HMSO). Published two years before the Plowden Report in England, the memorandum was advocating a new approach to teaching and learning in primary schools that was 'child-centred' and 'activity-based'. Underlying the thinking of the authors was the educational psychology of Jean Piaget, and the educational philosophy of Jean-Jacques Rousseau's *Émile*. They might also have suggested the educational work of Patrick Geddes.

Compare, for example, the following extracts on the ways in which children's thinking differs from adults; overall they show a remarkable conflation of ideas.

Primary Memorandum:

'She (the teacher) must realise that the child is not an adult in miniature: he does not feel, or act, or think like an adult. It is her function to supply means of assisting his natural development, and not to distort it by adopting a logical approach or by insisting too early on adult standards for which the child is not yet ready'.

Émile:

'Nature would have them children before they are men... Childhood has its own ways of seeing, thinking and feeling; nothing is more foolish than to try and substitute our ways'.

Patrick Geddes:

'Without at first obtruding map or even compass, he leads or rather follows his pupils as they wander through wood and brake, and linger by ferny bank and rushy pool. The beauty of the country, the natural interest in strange things and common ones, the questions they raise to the child's mind, not to the teacher's – here is the true stuff of nature study and of geography alike'.

Secondly, the author, Tom Masterton (1931-), was profoundly influenced by Patrick Geddes through his son, Arthur. Educated at Commercial School (headteacher – Norman Johnson), then Dunfermline High School and Edinburgh University, Masterton particularly remembers Dr Geddes's course on Monsoon Asia; reading the works of Tagore; as a post-graduate, assisting Dr Geddes with the preparation of his 1954 paper on 'Variability in change of population in the United States and Canada', and fruitful private discussions about the work and ideas of Patrick Geddes.

Although involved in writing and editing textbooks on a range of topics, and some sixty booklets in the popular Moray House series REST – *Resources for Environmental Studies Teaching* – the breadth of his Geddesian predilections is best expressed in 'Environmental Studies', which very effectively demonstrates not only his ability to cope with the interdisciplinary demands of the Primary Memorandum but from his own perception of geography – a geography that is an intellectual vagrant.

Fig 24 shows, for example, the potential links between maths, history, science, geography and art in a study of water. Finally, it is worth noting that all Masterton's work is enlivened by a proliferation of personally drawn and very striking maps, sketches and diagrams, further reinforcing the significance of visual education as an integral part of the Geddesian message.

Not all, however, were sympathetic to the methods of Regional Survey. LW Lyde (1863-1947) classicist and one-time geography teacher at Merchiston

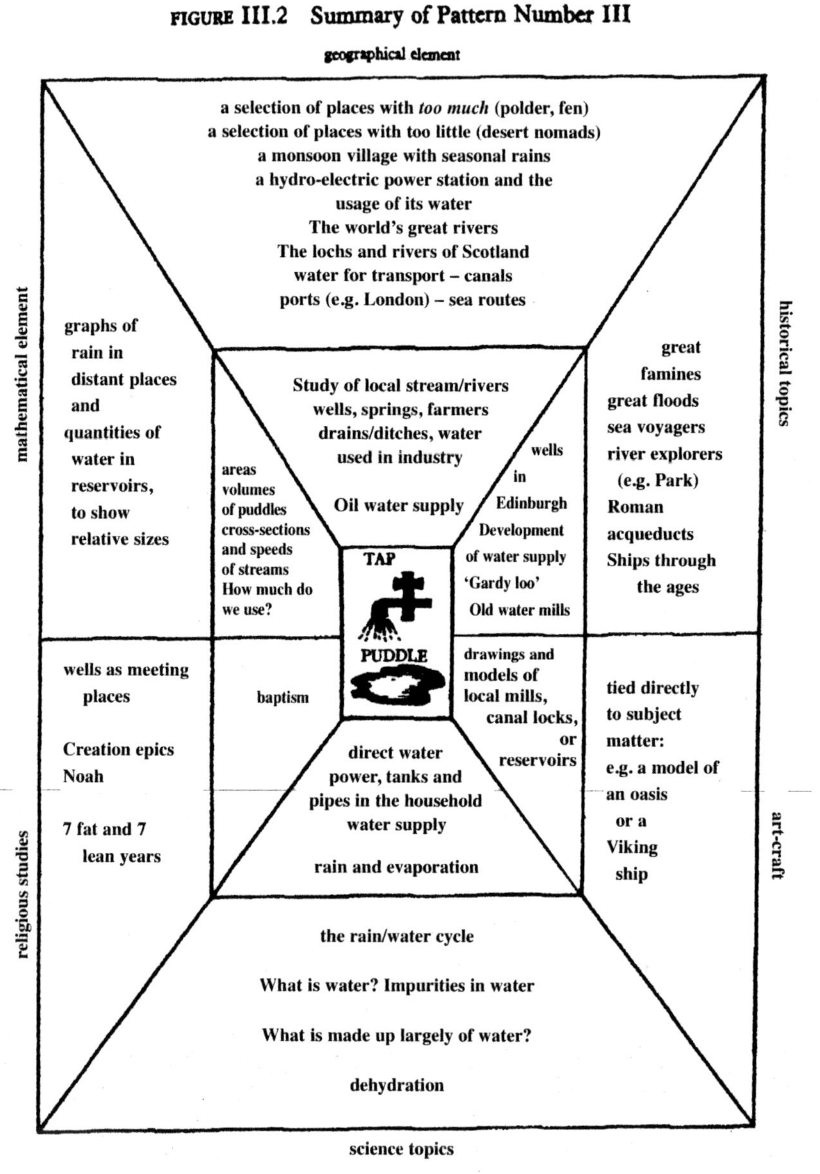

FIGURE III.2   Summary of Pattern Number III

geographical element

mathematical element

historical topics

religious studies

art-craft

a selection of places with *too much* (polder, fen)
a selection of places with too little (desert nomads)
a monsoon village with seasonal rains
a hydro-electric power station and the usage of its water
The world's great rivers
The lochs and rivers of Scotland
water for transport – canals
ports (e.g. London) – sea routes

graphs of rain in distant places and quantities of water in reservoirs, to show relative sizes

Study of local stream/rivers wells, springs, farmers drains/ditches, water used in industry

areas volumes of puddles cross-sections and speeds of streams How much do we use?

Oil water supply

wells in Edinburgh Development of water supply 'Gardy loo' Old water mills

TAP

great famines
great floods
sea voyagers
river explorers
(e.g. Park)
Roman acqueducts
Ships through the ages

PUDDLE

wells as meeting places

Creation epics
Noah

7 fat and 7 lean years

baptism

direct water power, tanks and pipes in the household water supply

rain and evaporation

drawings and models of local mills, canal locks, or reservoirs

tied directly to subject matter:
e.g. a model of an oasis or a Viking ship

the rain/water cycle

What is water? Impurities in water

What is made up largely of water?

dehydration

science topics

Fig. 24 An interdisciplinary approach to the study of water.
(T H Masterton)

School, Edinburgh, and later Professor of Geography at University College, London, was against outdoor geography because the boys 'regarded it as a picnic', and 'the road to knowledge' must not 'appear too easy'; while MacMunn (in *The Child's Path to Freedom*) quotes a ten-year old 'to begin with your own neighbourhood... might interest a few' but it prevented you from 'wanting to find out all about the world'. Such sentiments, however, were outweighed in schools and education colleges, as the ideals and methodology of regional survey – albeit variously nuanced – increasingly were adopted by classroom practitioners.

Regional Geography in the Classroom

Paralleling the increased vogue for Regional Survey was the mainly book-centred teaching of regional geography. Following Herbertson's leading role, texts proliferated in the inter-war period, derived from three sources:

other university lecturers such as L Dudley Stamp and Marion Newbigin (also editor of the *Scottish Geographical Magazine*);

geography specialists in education departments and colleges, notably Ayrshire-born James Fairgrieve, whose *Real Geography* series, written with London headteacher EW Young reached sales of over 400,000 by the 1960s;

an ever increasing number of geography teachers among whom Dorothy Preece, Thomas Pickles, Leonard Brookes and Jasper Stembridge were significant figures in England, and TS Muir and J Hamilton Birrell, north of the Border.

In varying styles, such texts 'packaged and repackaged the world's information in a variety of regional ways'. Frequently, though not always, continental areas were presented in a sequence: Southern Continents in younger years; then the more densely peopled (and therefore more complicated) North America and Asia, Europe and the British Isles. Equally, regions were presented, learned and regurgitated in a well-rehearsed sequence: position, relief, climate, natural vegetation, populations, occupations and settlement.

The Chairman of the PG Trust recalls how, under 'Tombstone' Campbell at a famous High School of Science and Technology, South America was studied by drawing up a vast table with the countries down the left side and the above headings along the top. A Thinking Machine? He thinks not! But it gave a feeling of satisfaction when complete.

Some approved of this particular regional approach. Scottish playwright, Liz Lochhead, looked back favourably to geography at Dalziel High School, Motherwell, in the early 1960s with her nicely deterministic statement that:

'Geography was marvellous. Logical. A revelation. Position, Climate, Natural Vegetation. It seemed to me maybe people were different because conditions were different. Something which had never occurred to me in twelve years'.

According to RC Honeybone, Head of Geography at the London Institute of Education, such an approach would not be deemed a true geographical synthesis, rather

'such regional accounts in school are mere feats of memory, with little or no relationship between the various parts.'

Something of the regional ordering of school geography also stuck with Richmal Crompton's incorrigible William and his Outlaws in their search for spies:

'Ginger: 'I've found the head of 'em. He's a big fat man with a red face an' a white moustache an' he's sittin' at a table lookin' at a map.'

'Well that *proves* it' said William equally excited, 'that *proves* it. If he wasn't foreign he wun't need to be lookin' at a map, would he? If he was really English like what they pretend to be he wun't need to be lookin' at a map of England. He'd've done England at school in Geography.' The Outlaws agreed that the logic of this was unassailable.'

William's confidence in regional geography was not matched by everyone. In his *Geography in British Schools 1850-2000*, Rex Walford heads his chapter on this period 'Regions and the Road to Ennui, 1940-60'. Not only was there the problem of a determinist interpretation, but

'there seemed little to excite the world at higher levels, no in-depth study of issues... few tools of analysis'. Effectively, 'the processes behind what was happening were as important as systematically laying out the pattern of things'. At its best, however, regional geography countered such criticisms, as textbooks from Honeybone and later authors such as Rex Beddis and Bill Marsden proved.

By the mid-1970s extensive areal coverage was avoided; in textbooks, use was made of focused sample studies of real 'folk' and real 'work' in farms, villages, squatter settlements, plantations or factories; the realities of 'place' were more effectively conveyed by integrating topographic maps – British and foreign – as illustrative of the areal context under consideration; extracts from newspapers, novels and travel books were employed; the use of photographs, slides, filmstrips and radiovision broadcasts were the norm, while the sounds of classroom discussions of contentious issues, simulations and games increasingly were heard.

As an illustration, Norman Thomson (1933-), then Principal Teacher of Geography at Broughton Secondary, Edinburgh, argued the '3Rs' approach to classroom teaching: material should be Real, Recent and Relevant.

Discussing a case study of Brunette Downs Cattle Station, Northern Territory, that used Australian large-scale, topographic maps, statistics demonstrating rainfall variability, filmstrips, and extracts culled from Mary Durack's *Kings in Grass Castles*, whose rich prose effectively conveyed the seasonality of 'place/work/ folk' in the outback, Thomson, while acknowledging the difficulties for pupils in making generalisations, persuasively showed the undoubted value of such in-depth studies set in their regional context.

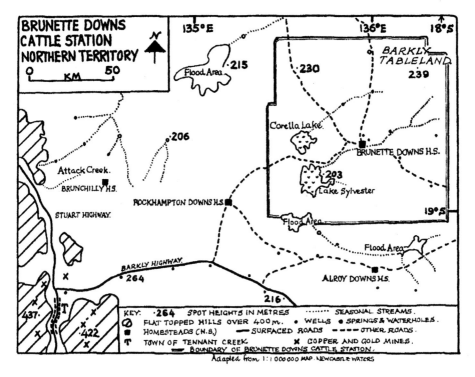

Fig. 25 Brunette Downs Cattle Station, Northern Territory.
A location map adapted from an Australian 1:1,000,000 map as part of a sample
study approach to geography teaching, illustrating the outback landscape.
(Norman Thomson)

Such classroom approaches had long been advocated; now they were
commonplace, and it was clear that 'traditional' regional geography had been
transformed. Potentially, a programme of effective classroom teaching of
'place/work/folk' could be organised within an area studies framework; an
approach that allowed concepts from systematic geography to be introduced
and reintroduced in a variety of areal contexts, thereby fostering a sense of
place – a common goal shared with the best traditions of regional survey in
the Geddesian mould but adapted to the classroom environment.

Conclusion

This assessment of Geddes and his views of Regional Survey and education
has illustrated the importance of selected 'disciples' in universities and schools,
discussing their roles as catalysts in spreading his ideas, particularly after

1918. Although often seen by some historians of the subject as 'a geographical Dark age, part of a dull interlude between the aggressive period of exploration and empire and the conquest of a spatial science,' revisionist thinking suggests that the inter-war years were enlivened by Geddes and other protagonists of Regional Survey. As discussed, it was more than just a fostering of local knowledge; it was aimed at educating the future citizens through a regional, synthetic approach to a range of geographical issues, not least those of the expanding cities of Britain. But it embraced more than just the local, it was equally national and global in outlook, educating everyone 'to be at once a local, national and world citizen'. Perhaps Geddes himself best summed up such an outlook in the following excerpt from Perth Academy school magazine, *The Young Barbarian*, advocating a life-long, educational programme fashioned from the perspective of Regional Survey:

'If my tale requires a moral... mine is simple enough. Don't be satisfied with lessons, or even with books, delightful as they are; nor with games and sports either; but see all you can of the world for yourself, since that is what books are about. Ramble and roam; yet not as a mere tourist, a 'globe trotter'. Observe and understand how people live and work; and this may be by sharing in their work and life, from hills down to sea and back again... Get into active survey, always growing out and extending, of the real world around you. And be seeking out, and finding out, what your life can best do to help in that, to be of service to it.'

A Letter from India

Narayani Gupta

Department of History and Culture
Jamia Millia Islamia
New Delhi

Dear Dr Stephen,

I WAS DELIGHTED TO receive your invitation. How thoughtful to celebrate Geddes on Mahatma Gandhi's birth anniversary, I thought. It took me some moments to realize that 2nd October was also Patrick Geddes's birthday! There is something appropriate in the fact that these two men, who had many points of similarity, should share a birthday.

As we approach 2nd October, Geddes Jayanti (*jayanti = anniversary*), I look back on my thirty years' acquaintance with him. I first came across him in the volume of essays in honour of Mumbai's first Professor of Sociology. Soon after, Helen Meller came out to India to locate any clues Geddes might have left in libraries in India. Many years later, in 1988, I followed my own Geddes trail to Edinburgh, and met the charming Percy Johnson-Marshall, Sofia Leonard and Benjamin Tindall. Talking to them made me realise that Geddes had a strong presence in Scotland as well as in India!

What does Geddes mean for India? Why do Indian scholars from disciplines as disparate as anthropology and architecture get excited by his ideas? Perhaps because he was individual enough, in a time of increasing specialisation, to believe that subjects should not be sealed off from each other, and because he was blessed with a tireless curiosity to learn.

'Only connect' said his contemporary, EM Forster. Geddes did just that. He is special for us because he was one of the middlemen, like CF Andrews, Edward Thompson and Annie Besant, who linked two cultures, who talked to Indians as equals, not as subordinates.

He came to India at an extraordinarily significant moment. Historians have highlighted how the nationalist movement gained a new vigour under Gandhi's leadership. It was a movement sustained not just by impatience and grievances, but also by the vision of an exhilarating future. It was at this time that Muhammad Iqbal wrote the poem beginning '*Saare jahan se achha*', a song familiar to every Indian child. It was a period of increased interaction between people and ideas. It was a time of idealism, of preparing blueprints for a future where the best of Indian tradition would be linked to the best of Western institutions. There was a sense of confidence at the potential of Indian music and dance forms and literatures, in the ability of Indians to make a contribution to Western science. It is not surprising that among Geddes's friends were men of music and literature, like Rabindranath Tagore, as well as scientists like Jagdish Bose.

To the aspects of Indian tradition to be celebrated, Geddes added one – townscapes. Beauty in India, he said, was not only stunning natural land-scapes but also the skyline and groundline of its towns. Indian towns had been admired and described in earlier centuries, but hardly any European in the nineteenth or twentieth century had had a good word for them. Their implicit disapproval had rubbed off on Indians. And now, here was this truly amazing development – a scholar who was an authority on the history of European towns was expressing his appreciation of *our* towns!

Geddes saw things that other people, frazzled by the large numbers of people and the noise in Indian streets, did not notice. At a time when orderly 'town-planning' was becoming fashionable, this man from Edinburgh found a kindred spirit in the crowded Indian towns. What a contrast to the patent disapproval expressed by his contemporary, EP Richards, compiling a long list of 'improvements' for Calcutta. To the characters in EM Forster's *Passage to India*, written at the time Geddes was wandering in India, Indian crowds were intimidating. Geddes found them lively and interesting. Katherine Mayo wrote fastidiously about the deplorable Indian practices at the time of childbirth. Geddes was fascinated by the colour and laughter of clusters of Indian women, and the informal spaces they created. Lowell Thomas shuddered at the world-liness sculpted on the walls of some Indian temples, but Geddes marvelled at the beauty of what he called 'temple cities', a term that was to endure. While the colonial government was seeking to define its relations with Indian princes, Geddes was designing an extension for Indore, the capital of an Indian 'princely state' .

I am convinced that if Geddes had not happened to India, we would have had little sense today of the old Indian discourse on architecture and planning. Well after Geddes had left India, modern Indian architecture was to take off in a swift soaring movement drawing from the fount of Western modernism. These young Indian architects and planners, proudly wearing their degrees from American and European universities like medals, did not cast a glance backward. But in the 1920s, Geddes's enthusiasm had galvanised many scholars of Sanskrit (who were not necessarily interested in architecture) to translate the surviving *Silpasastra* and *Vaastusastra*, treatises on town-building and on the norms of architecture dating back to the fifth century AD. This is India's greatest debt to Geddes, the kind of debt we owe to Fergusson or Prinsep.

What we could well relearn from Geddes is his habit of spending more time out-of-doors than in conference-rooms or at the drawing-board, and his belief that one must live among the people for whom one is designing a habitat. One cannot plan people's dwellings and the streets they must traverse unless one experiences the heat of the midday sun or the devastation a monsoon torrent can cause.

To Geddes, friendly curving lanes, compact buildings and a low skyline were the ingredients of a non-threatening town. He would have enjoyed the popular genre of Urdu poems that celebrate the conviviality generated by the *gali*, the *culs-de-sac* typical of north Indian towns. He was horrified by the arrogance of Edwin Lutyens' blueprint for New Delhi, and urged that its axis be swung in an anticlockwise sense, to connect with the adjacent Mughal city of Delhi instead of looking away from it. Planners in India after Independence imbibed two doctrines which worked in North America, where land was plentiful and older towns non-existent – the grid-pattern for streets and the generous estates allocated for public buildings. But today, as our towns get saturated, the relevance of Geddes's philosophy and his suggestions for 'conservative surgery' acquire a new relevance. We need to bring him back.

Patrick Geddes – the Legacy

Walter Stephen

THE WORLDS OF PATRICK GEDDES by Philip Boardman has a hypnotic caricature of PG on the cover with a list of his attributes – Biologist, Town Planner, Re-educator, Peace-warrior. The other contributors to this book each start with a list at least as long, but sometimes more diverse. Geddes saw himself as a 'comprehensive, synthesising generalist' who always tried to 'see life whole'. His family found him lovable and a tyrant. To his friends he was a source of vital inspiration and utterly exasperating. On his very first page, Boardman, who led the discontented students of the Scots College in Montpellier, says:

'Turn by turn – and even simultaneously – he was a botanist, economist, sociologist, producer of pageants, public lecturer, writer of verse, art critic, publisher, civic reformer, town planner, Victorian moralist, provocative agnostic and academic revolutionary.'

Boardman's last chapter ('Patrick Geddes Today') makes depressing reading. 'Today' being 1978, he begins by going through Geddes's practical projects and finds, unsurprisingly, that most have foundered or lost their original purpose. The Outlook Tower has lost its educational direction and, after housing the Patrick Geddes Centre for Planning Studies, now functions as a tourist attraction. Like Short's Observatory before Geddes, it's focus is on light, and is science-related. Riddle's Court, the first self-governing students' hostel in Europe, fell into the hands of the City of Edinburgh's Education Department and was put to a Geddes-like use as a centre for Community Education and the Workers' Education Association. Now, however, it is to be sold off, one reason being its unsuitability for the disabled. Walking down Johnston Terrace, the area of flat ground which became the garden of Castlehill School seems an overgrown wilderness. Ramsay Lodge was sold off to the Commercial Bank of Scotland (later the National Commercial and later still, the Royal) as a hostel and training centre.

Abroad, Sofia Leonard has shown us the disparity between the plans of Geddes for Indian cities and the actuality on the ground. Cyprus? Geddes left the execution of his recommendations to local interests more interested in short-term gain and ethnic strife than the necessarily long-term green revolution he advocated. Jerusalem? A truly international university, an old Arab quarter respected and integrated with new additions – how could these survive the turbulence of the British Mandate and the emergence of the state of Israel? It was a Zionist who said 'there are few who could rise to the lofty heights of his imagination and practical knowledge'. The Scots College, under-capitalised and on the margin, struggled on in the shadows. Lilian, Geddes's widow, subsidised it until the Second World War, when it passed through the hands of Vichy, the Germans and the liberated French. Post-war it housed handicapped children.

Yet the picture is not so bleak and the legacy is greater than might be supposed at first inspection. A century on, the Work-Place-Folk of our time is not the Work-Place-Folk of Geddes's. In the eighteenth and nineteenth centuries the well-to-do deserted the Old Town for the New, leaving the poor to rot in the ancient slums. In the twentieth century the poor have had their revenge and have deserted (or been decanted) to the new suburbs. In 1951 the school-aged population of St Giles Ward (the Old Town) was 2,712 and by 1971 it was 880. Result – school closures, no street life, no community in the Geddes's sense and so on.

By example and through his building ventures Geddes started to lure the middle classes back into the Old Town. In 1948 White Horse Close was old, very picturesque – and badly run down. Now it is even older but neat and clean and tidy – some might say gentrified. Instead of the beauty of decay and the intimation of mortality we have the geometric play of light and shade on sharp, clear surfaces and the cheerful colours of window boxes. Clearly the Folk of the Old Town are not the same Folk as 100 years ago.

In 1960, within 50 yards of Deacon Brodie's pub, there were two horticultural shops, one on either side, selling tools, seeds, fertilisers and, in season, bedding plants and vegetables for planting out. Where have all the flowers gone? To the bypass, every one! Behind the street-line, up closes and in little workshops were blacksmiths and other metalworkers. Work has changed dramatically, now seeming to consist mainly of selling tartan scarves and sandwiches.

What of Place? In 1913 there were 588 properties with 'sanitary defects' in St Giles Ward. Old photographs show us how picturesque it all was, old photographs also show us scores of barefoot children having their free school meals in North Canongate School. 'The death of the fine-grained city' describes the 'sixties treatment, *au Haussmann*, of large chunks of Edinburgh, and the Old Town has its share, but the main visual impact is of gaudy, non-traditional shopfronts taking over the pavements.

In this new Work-Place-Folk triad the hand of Geddes is still traceable. Ramsay Garden crowns the Old Town ridge superbly. In the Geddes Flat Robert Naismith and his sister Anne lived for twenty-five years, restoring 13 of the 22 murals Geddes had had painted there. Robert Naismith was an architect and planner of some distinction and a partner in Sir Frank Mears Associates, the firm founded by Geddes's son-in-law and co-worker. The circle was completed when the flat was bequeathed to the National Trust for Scotland.

The Trust are planning to perform a sensitive upgrade of the flat, while retaining its highly significant character. The accompanying gift of some very significant pieces of furniture will be kept within the flat in their original settings – again maintaining the feel and character of the history of the place. Once

Fig. 26 The Geddes Flat in Ramsay Garden

Robert Naismith and his sister Annie in their first-floor Geddes flat in Ramsay Garden. After living in it for twenty-five years and partly restoring it, they bequeathed the flat to the National Trust for Scotland.
(Scotsman Publications)

this work is done, the Trust will look via a letting agent for sympathetic tenants to live in and love the flat.

Milne's Court (Plate 1a) was built in 1690 and refurbished by Geddes as a student hostel. The Saltire Society in 1971 carried on the practice of conservative surgery by re-restoring the building as an university hostel. Geddes would have approved. James Court, where the young marrieds set up home among the near-slum dwellers, has come through a period of near-dereliction and is now a pleasant off-street oasis with healthy trees.

Labour costs and changing taste mean that public gardens today differ markedly from those of PG's time. Everything in the Castlehill School garden (Fig 3) was stiff – stiff collars on the boys, girls in stiff skirts, vegetables and flowers in stiff rows. What we may have thought waste ground in Johnston Terrace is not waste at all – it is a wildlife garden created by the Worldwide Fund for Nature to ensure our native plants and animals have a place in the city centre (Plate 8a). A garden for Geddes's time has evolved into a garden for ours.

Heavily influenced by Geddes, the Senior Adviser in Lothian Region Education Department took the view that Edinburgh was the best place (in Western Europe) for a young person to grow up in, and the best place for learning about it was as near the Castle as one could get. An Environmental Studies Curriculum for the primary schools specified a major topic of study for Primary 7 as 'Growth of the City' (a wider concept than the growth of Edinburgh). Concerned that the Outlook Tower could not function as an 'educational laboratory' he established in Cannonball House Britain's first successful Urban Studies Centre. (Cannonball House was an annexe of Castlehill School, which closed when the roll collapsed).

Staffed initially under the government's Job Creation Scheme and then by Lothian Region, Castlehill Urban Studies Centre was, in effect, a re-creation of the Geddes Outlook Tower. Classes would visit the centre, which was fitted out with a range of briefing and learning media. They would then sally forth, under guidance, to observe and record and do all the good things that Kenneth Maclean describes in his contribution. The great advantage the centre had was that the field experience was part of the local authority structure and work done at Castlehill could be developed further back at school. For twenty years Castlehill was the focus for purposeful and inspirational activity.

When we consider the legacy of Patrick Geddes, two words spring to mind – example and inspiration. It is easy to pay lip-service to the educational triad of Head, Heart and Hand, but Geddes repeatedly showed that he meant it. The first of his three doves, as Murdo Macdonald reminds us, was Sympathy, which meant for Geddes getting right into the problem, or area, or community. He acquired sympathy by carrying out surveys, walking the streets, talking to the locals. Not for him the blank white paper on the drawing-board, for him a project began with Work. In James Court he led the painters, in his final years he was shifting stones at the Scots College. Hear the contempt when he said – 'Aha! Look at them – how clean and white and useless: the hands of a paper-gentleman'.

In 1819 the Poet Laureate, Robert Southey, accompanied Thomas Telford on what was for Telford a working tour of Scotland. Wrote Southey:

'Telford's is a happy life: everywhere making roads, building bridges, forming canals, and creating harbours – works of sure, solid, permanent utility; every-where employing a great number of persons, selecting the most meritorious, and putting them forward in the world, in his own way.'

Telford's legacy is still with us, neat, strong, handsome and useful. Thousands of commuters daily cross the Dean Bridge into Edinburgh's West End without a thought of the mighty arches spanning the Water of Leith. Similarly, Telford's splendid A68 is now a racetrack where speeding motorists are oblivious to the inspiring viaduct they use to cross the Tyne valley. The Caledonian Canal and the Shropshire canals are visible and still in use. The Menai Bridge and Craigellachie may have been sidelined by a century and a half and more of heavier and faster traffic, but each still forms an impressive element of its setting. Inverness has its Telford Road, Edinburgh its Telford College and Shropshire its New Town. Telford's legacy is there for us all to see and touch and admire, if we so choose.

By contrast, if we think back to the few examples of the Geddes legacy mentioned earlier it is clear that there was no direct transmission from the time of Geddes to our own. This is what so depressed Boardman, that very little seemed to have survived. Even in his lifetime Geddes was a maverick. For example, he and Lutyens in India could not have been further apart – and both said so! After his death his star sunk even lower and we were into the era of the machine for living and the grandiose solution. But Geddes's legacy is a legacy of the mind and because of this it could wither away – as it almost did. But like the leaves he admired so much, when conditions improved and people's minds became disillusioned or receptive to seemingly new ideas, there was a flush of new growth of interest in his thinking.

It seems small beer now, but some may remember the post-war Labour Government's Groundnut Scheme and the furore it caused – for the wrong reasons. There was a worldwide shortage of fats and oils post-Second World War and the government devised a huge scheme for growing groundnuts in what was then Tanganyika (now Tanzania). The scheme was a disaster, everything was wrong or went wrong and £39 million was wasted. Peanuts by today's standards but scandalous then! However, public opinion got the wrong end of the stick and blamed the government for wasting money. The blame should have gone to those who were negligent by planning on the big scale in abstract. A Geddes plan would have been tiresome, unspectacular and fiddly – but it could have produced the goods.

In recent years Geddes has made a comeback, he has become an inspirational figure. We know that Captain Geddes encouraged Patrick's reading, which was always worthy and voracious. Perhaps modelling himself on Carlyle, another serious lad from a modest background who rose to command a world audience, Patrick developed a prose style which did not please either the *Times Literary Supplement* or the *Manchester Guardian*. 'An unfortunate dialect', said the *Guardian*. Said the former:

'O for one hour of Swift or Newton! O for one hour of almost anybody who has learned to write a Latin prose!'

Yet, at the same time, Geddes was able to find a concise description of a process – 'conservative surgery' – or a method – 'impact anonymous', or to produce the quotable quote. A voluminous writer, his dense style made sure he would never be a bestseller. 'Every schoolboy knows' Sir Thomas More's *Utopia* or Erasmus's *In Praise of Folly* but Geddes wrote nothing of the kind.

Even as a speaker he could scarcely be heard at times and what was heard could be repetitious or, sometimes, tangential. Yet, somehow, despite all this, Geddes-type activities are going on without any direct input from the great man.

Kenneth Maclean reminded us of the Dunfermline Plan, which was never implemented. Yet he is able to describe a web of educational activity around Dunfermline which grew from – what? Not the plan, but from a much vaguer understanding, almost a folk memory, of what was right, what was best for the learners.

In Moliere's *Le Bourgeois Gentilhomme* there comes a moment when the central character – hardly a hero – suddenly discovers all his life he has been talking Prose and gets quite excited about it. Many of us today are like that in relation to Geddes. So often we think of an issue – and he has been there and tested it. We drive through a strange town and see a nice suburb and then realise that what makes it nice is that it could have been laid out by Geddes.

The legacy of Geddes is a legacy of the mind. Thus Geddes it was who coined the mantra 'Think Global, Act Local' (in *Cities in Evolution* in 1915) – although most of us would have guessed it emerged from Rio about 1994. It is very easy to think about the big picture – although few of us can do so with any originality. Acting locally is now very difficult for most of us. Geddes set us an example by acting locally when he could and using this to illuminate the big ideas which could transform society – which would usually be done by acting locally. So it goes on – example, then inspiration, example again, then... and so on.

Almost the last word in Boardman's book lies with Pheroze R Bharucha, whose photograph we saw near the beginning of this book. He knew Geddes when he was towards the end of his life, in his late seventies and, presumably, fading away.

'He inspired you: he brought the best out of you: he re-kindled the creative spark in you. It is as a Teacher that he will live in our hearts and memories....

'Assuredly there have been very few like him – they hardly come once in a century. He just set you on fire with love of this earth and with desire to cleanse it, to beautify and re-beautify it, to build and re-build it...

'What was the secret of Geddes's amazing activity? What was his inspiration? It was, we believe, an unbounded love for the human kind with all its faults. No poet, prophet or theologian has regarded man as verily created in the image of God with a clearer perception, with more absolute certainty of conviction than Patrick Geddes.'

Chronology

1854	Born 2 October, in Ballater, youngest of five children
1857	Family moved to Mount Tabor, Perth
1871	Left Perth Academy for work in bank and 'free home studies'
1874	Biology at Edinburgh (one week) and London (under Huxley)
1878	Roscoff (Brittany) and the Sorbonne
1879	The Mexican adventure
1880	Demonstrator in Botany, Edinburgh University
1886	Marriage to Anna Morton
1887	Norah Geddes born
	University Hall, first self-governing hostel
1887-1900	Summer schools set up and run every August
1888	Professor of Botany, University College, Dundee
1891	Alasdair Geddes born
1892	Outlook Tower started
1893	Ramsay Garden created as co-operative flats
1895	Arthur Geddes born
1897	Cyprus – survey and planning
1900	Held International Assembly at Exposition Universelle, Paris
	First visit to United States
1901	Return visit to USA
1903	Dunfermline development plan and publication of *City Development*
1908	Crosby Hall (Chelsea) relocated and restored as residence for university women
1910	Cities Exhibition at Chelsea, then toured until lost at sea 1914
1913	Cities Exhibition awarded Grand Prix in Ghent
1914-15	First visit to India (with Alasdair)
1915	*Cities in Evolution* published
1915-17	Second visit to India (with Anna)
1917	Deaths of Alasdair and Anna
1919	Retirement and Farewell Lecture (Dundee)
	Planning in Jerusalem and Tel Aviv
	Professor of Civics and Sociology at Bombay
1919-23	Third visit to India (with Arthur)
1923	Third visit to USA
1924	Left Bombay for Montpellier (health reasons)
	Collège des Écossais founded
1925	Civil List pension of £80 awarded

1926	Compensation of £2,000 paid for loss of Cities Exhibition
	Geddes's Plan for city of Tel Aviv officially accepted
1928	Marriage to Lilian Brown
1932	Offer of knighthood accepted – accolade 25 February
1932	Death at Montpellier – 17 April
1962	*Silent Spring* – Rachel Carson
1972	'Blueprint for Survival' – *The Economist*
1973	Establishment of Sir Patrick Geddes Memorial Trust
	'Geddes-Awareness' campaign started by *Bulletin of Environmental Education*
1974	*Small is Beautiful: Economics as if People Mattered* – EF Schumacher
1975	*A Most Unsettling Person* – Paddy Kitchen
1978	*The Worlds of Patrick Geddes* – Patrick Boardman
1982	Commemorative events in several locations, home and abroad
1985	Patrick Geddes Centre for Planning Studies set up (in the Outlook Tower)
1990	*Patrick Geddes: Social Evolutionist and City Planner* – Helen Meller
1991-92	International Summer Meetings run by Patrick Geddes Centre
1992	Rio Earth Summit and Local Agenda 21
2004	Geddes 150th Anniversary Symposium: Ideas in Evolution, Edinburgh
	Geddes Garden at Scots College in Montpellier restored
	Anniversary Exhibition at The Matthew Gallery, University of Edinburgh – Patrick Geddes: The Regeneration of Edinburgh

Select Bibliography

A Most Unsettling Person, Paddy Kitchen (Victor Gollancz Ltd, 1975)

The Worlds of Patrick Geddes, Philip Boardman (Routledge and Kegan Paul, 1978)

The Buildings of Scotland: Edinburgh, Gifford, MacWilliam and Walker (Penguin Books Ltd, 1984)

Patrick Geddes: Social Evolutionist and City Planner, Helen Meller (Routledge, 1990)

Patrick Geddes: Ecologist, Educator, Visual Thinker, Murdo Macdonald (ed), (Edinburgh Review, Issue 88, Summer 1992)

The Regeneration of the Old Town of Edinburgh by Patrick Geddes, Sofia Leonard (Planning History Vol 21 No 2, February 1999)

Some other books published by **LUATH** PRESS
published from Scotland, read around the world

NATURAL WORLD

The Hydro Boys: pioneers of renewable energy
Emma Wood
ISBN 1 84282 047 8 PB £8.99

Wild Scotland
James McCarthy
photographs by Laurie Campbell
ISBN 0 946487 37 5 PB £8.99

Wild Lives: Otters – On the Swirl of the Tide
Bridget MacCaskill
ISBN 0 946487 67 7 PB £9.99

Wild Lives: Foxes – The Blood is Wild
Bridget MacCaskill
ISBN 0 946487 71 5 PB £9.99

Scotland – Land & People: An Inhabited Solitude
James McCarthy
ISBN 0 946487 57 X PB £7.99

The Highland Geology Trail
John L Roberts
ISBN 0 946487 36 7 PB £5.99

Red Sky at Night
John Barrington
ISBN 0 946487 60 X PB £8.99

Listen to the Trees
Don MacCaskill
ISBN 0 946487 65 0 PB £9.99

THE QUEST FOR

The Quest for the Celtic Key
Karen Ralls-MacLeod and
Ian Robertson
ISBN 0 946487 73 1 HB £18.99
ISBN 1 84282 031 1 PB £8.99

The Quest for Arthur
Stuart McHardy
ISBN 1 84282 012 5 HB £16.99

The Quest for the Nine Maidens
Stuart McHardy
ISBN 0 946487 66 9 HB £16.99

The Quest for Charles Rennie Mackintosh
John Cairney
ISBN 1 84282 058 3 HB £16.99

The Quest for Robert Louis Stevenson
John Cairney
ISBN 0 946487 87 1 HB £16.99

The Quest for the Original Horse Whisperers
Russell Lyon
ISBN 1 84282 020 6 HB £16.99

ON THE TRAIL OF

On the Trail of the Pilgrim Fathers
J. Keith Cheetham
ISBN 0 946487 83 9 PB £7.99

On the Trail of Mary Queen of Scots
J. Keith Cheetham
ISBN 0 946487 50 2 PB £7.99

On the Trail of John Wesley
J. Keith Cheetham
ISBN 1 84282 023 0 PB £7.99

On the Trail of William Wallace
David R. Ross
ISBN 0 946487 47 2 PB £7.99

On the Trail of Robert the Bruce
David R. Ross
ISBN 0 946487 52 9 PB £7.99

On the Trail of Robert Service
GW Lockhart
ISBN 0 946487 24 3 PB £7.99

On the Trail of John Muir
Cherry Good
ISBN 0 946487 62 6 PB £7.99

On the Trail of Robert Burns
John Cairney
ISBN 0 946487 51 0 PB £7.99

On the Trail of Bonnie Prince Charlie
David R Ross
ISBN 0 946487 68 5 PB £7.99

On the Trail of Queen Victoria in the Highlands
Ian R Mitchell
ISBN 0 946487 79 0 PB £7.99

ISLANDS

The Islands that Roofed the World: Easdale, Belnahua, Luing & Seil:
Mary Withall
ISBN 0 946487 76 6 PB £4.99

Rum: Nature's Island
Magnus Magnusson
ISBN 0 946487 32 4 PB £7.95

LUATH GUIDES TO SCOTLAND

The North West Highlands: Roads to the Isles
Tom Atkinson
ISBN 0 946487 54 5 PB £4.95

Mull and Iona: Highways and Byways
Peter Macnab
ISBN 0 946487 58 8 PB £4.95

The Northern Highlands: The Empty Lands
Tom Atkinson
ISBN 0 946487 55 3   PB £4.95

The West Highlands: The Lonely Lands
Tom Atkinson
ISBN 0 946487 56 1 PB £4.95

South West Scotland
Tom Atkinson
ISBN 0 946487 04 9 PB £4.95

TRAVEL & LEISURE

Die Kleine Schottlandfibel [Scotland Guide in German]
Hans-Walter Arends
ISBN 0 946487 89 8 PB £8.99

Let's Explore Berwick-upon-Tweed
Anne Bruce English
ISBN 1 84282 029 X PB £4.99

Let's Explore Edinburgh Old Town
Anne Bruce English
ISBN 0 946487 98 7 PB £4.99

Edinburgh's Historic Mile
Duncan Priddle
ISBN 0 946487 97 9 PB £2.99

Pilgrims in the Rough: St Andrews beyond the 19th hole
Michael Tobert
ISBN 0 946487 74 X PB £7.99

FOOD & DRINK

The Whisky Muse: Scotch whisky in poem & song
various, compiled and edited by Robin Laing
ISBN 1 84282 041 9 PB £7.99

First Foods Fast: how to prepare good simple meals for your baby
Lara Boyd
ISBN 1 84282 002 8 PB £4.99

Edinburgh and Leith Pub Guide
Stuart McHardy
ISBN 0 946487 80 4 PB £4.95

WALK WITH LUATH

Skye 360: walking the coastline of Skye
Andrew Dempster
ISBN 0 946487 85 5 PB £8.99

Walks in the Cairngorms
Ernest Cross
ISBN 0 946487 09 X PB £4.95

Short Walks in the Cairngorms
Ernest Cross
ISBN 0 946487 23 5 PB £4.95

The Joy of Hillwalking
Ralph Storer
ISBN 0 946487 28 6 PB £7.50

Scotland's Mountains before the Mountaineers
Ian R Mitchell
ISBN 0 946487 39 1 PB £9.99

Mountain Days & Bothy Nights
Dave Brown & Ian R Mitchell
ISBN 0 946487 15 4 PB £7.50

BIOGRAPHY

The Last Lighthouse
Sharma Krauskopf
ISBN 0 946487 96 0 PB £7.99

Tobermory Teuchter
Peter Macnab
ISBN 0 946487 41 3 PB £7.99

Bare Feet & Tackety Boots
Archie Cameron
ISBN 0 946487 17 0 PB £7.95

Come Dungeons Dark
John Taylor Caldwell
ISBN 0 946487 19 7 PB £6.95

SOCIAL HISTORY

Pumpherston: the story of a shale oil village
Sybil Cavanagh
ISBN 1 84282 011 7 HB £17.99
ISBN 1 84282 015 X PB £10.99

Shale Voices
Alistair Findlay
ISBN 0 946487 78 2 HB £17.99
ISBN 0 946487 63 4 PB £10.99

A Word for Scotland
Jack Campbell
ISBN 0 946487 48 0 PB £12.99

Crofting Years
Francis Thompson
ISBN 0 946487 06 5 PB £6.95

HISTORY

Desire Lines: A Scottish Odyssey
David R Ross
ISBN 1 84282 033 8 PB £9.99

Civil Warrior: extraordinary life & poems of Montrose
Robin Bell
ISBN 1 84282 013 3 HB £10.99

FOLKLORE

Scotland: Myth, Legend & Folklore
Stuart McHardy
ISBN 0 946487 69 3 PB £7.99

Luath Storyteller: Highland Myths & Legends
George W Macpherson
ISBN 1 84282 003 6 PB £5.00

Tales of the North Coast
Alan Temperley
ISBN 0 946487 18 9 PB £8.99

Tall Tales from an Island
Peter Macnab
ISBN 0 946487 07 3 PB £8.99

The Supernatural Highlands
Francis Thompson
ISBN 0 946487 31 6 PB £8.99

GENEALOGY

Scottish Roots: step-by-step guide for ancestor hunters
Alwyn James
ISBN 1 84282 007 9 PB £9.99

SPORT

Over the Top with the Tartan Army
Andy McArthur
ISBN 0 946487 45 6 PB £7.99

Ski & Snowboard Scotland
Hilary Parke
ISBN 0 946487 35 9 PB £6.99

FICTION

The Road Dance
John MacKay
ISBN 1 84282 040 0 PB £6.99

Milk Treading
Nick Smith
ISBN 1 84282 037 0 PB £6.99

The Strange Case of RL Stevenson
Richard Woodhead
ISBN 0 946487 86 3 HB £16.99

But n Ben A-Go-Go
Matthew Fitt
ISBN 0 946487 82 0 HB £10.99
ISBN 1 84282 014 1 PB £6.99

Grave Robbers
Robin Mitchell
ISBN 0 946487 72 3 PB £7.99

The Bannockburn Years
William Scott
ISBN 0 946487 34 0 PB £7.95

The Great Melnikov
Hugh MacLachlan
ISBN 0 946487 42 1 PB £7.95

The Fundamentals of New Caledonia
David Nicol
ISBN 0 946487 93 6 HB £16.99

Heartland
John MacKay
ISBN 1 84282 059 1 PB £9.99

Driftnet
Lin Anderson
ISBN 1 84282 034 6 PB £9.99

Torch
Lin Anderson
ISBN 1 84282 042 7 PB £9.99

The Blue Moon Book
Anne Macleod
ISBN 1 84282 061 3 PB £9.99

The Glasgow Dragon
Des Dillon
ISBN 1 84282 056 7 PB £9.99

Six Black Candles [B format edition]
Des Dillon
ISBN 1 84282 053 2 PB £6.99

Me and Ma Gal [B format edition]
Des Dillon
ISBN 1 84282 054 0 PB £5.99

The Golden Menagerie
Allan Cameron
ISBN 1 84282 057 5 PB £9.99

POETRY

Drink the Green Fairy
Brian Whittingham
ISBN 1 84282 045 1 PB £8.99

The Ruba'iyat of Omar Khayyam, in Scots
Rab Wilson
ISBN 1 84282 046 X PB £8.99 (book)
ISBN 1 84282 070 2 £9.99 (audio CD)

Talking with Tongues
Brian Finch
ISBN 1 84282 006 0 PB £8.99

Kate o Shanter's Tale and other poems
Matthew Fitt
ISBN 1 84282 028 1 PB £6.99 (book)
ISBN 1 84282 043 5 £9.99 (audio CD)

Bad Ass Raindrop
Kokumo Rocks
ISBN 1 84282 018 4 PB £6.99

Madame Fi Fi's Farewell and other poems
Gerry Cambridge
ISBN 1 84282 005 2 PB £8.99

Scots Poems to be Read Aloud
Introduced by Stuart McHardy
ISBN 0 946487 81 2 PB £5.00

Picking Brambles and other poems
Des Dillon
ISBN 1 84282 021 4 PB £6.99

Sex, Death & Football
Alistair Findlay
ISBN 1 84282 022 2 PB £6.99

Tartan & Turban
Bashabi Fraser
ISBN 1 84282 044 3 PB £8.99

Immortal Memories: A Compilation of Toasts to the Memory of Burns as delivered at Burns Suppers, 1801-2001
John Cairney
ISBN 1 84282 009 5 HB £20.00

Poems to be Read Aloud
Introduced by Tom Atkinson
ISBN 0 946487 00 6 PB £5.00

Men and Beasts: wild men and tame animals
Valerie Gillies and Rebecca Marr
ISBN 0 946487 92 8 PB £15.00

Caledonian Cramboclink: the Poetry of
William Neill
ISBN 0 946487 53 7 PB £8.99

The Luath Burns Companion
John Cairney
ISBN 1 84282 000 1 PB £10.00

LANGUAGE

Luath Scots Language Learner [Book]
L Colin Wilson
ISBN 0 946487 91 X PB £9.99

Luath Scots Language Learner [Double Audio CD Set]
L Colin Wilson
ISBN 1 84282 026 5 CD £16.99

DETAILS OF ALL THE ABOVE BOOKS CAN BE FOUND AT
www.**luath**.co.uk

Luath Press Limited
committed to publishing well written books worth reading

LUATH PRESS takes its name from Robert Burns, whose little collie Luath (*Gael.*, swift or nimble) tripped up Jean Armour at a wedding and gave him the chance to speak to the woman who was to be his wife and the abiding love of his life. Burns called one of *The Twa Dogs* Luath after Cuchullin's hunting dog in *Ossian's Fingal*. Luath Press was established in 1981 in the heart of Burns country, and is now based a few steps up the road from Burns' first lodgings on Edinburgh's Royal Mile.

Luath offers you distinctive writing with a hint of unexpected pleasures.

Most bookshops in the UK, the US, Canada, Australia, New Zealand and parts of Europe either carry our books in stock or can order them for you. To order direct from us, please send a £sterling cheque, postal order, international money order or your credit card details (number, address of cardholder and expiry date) to us at the address below. Please add post and packing as follows: UK – £1.00 per delivery address; overseas surface mail – £2.50 per delivery address; overseas airmail – £3.50 for the first book to each delivery address, plus £1.00 for each additional book by airmail to the same address. If your order is a gift, we will happily enclose your card or message at no extra charge.

Luath Press Limited
543/2 Castlehill
The Royal Mile
Edinburgh EH1 2ND
Scotland
Telephone: 0131 225 4326 (24 hours)
Fax: 0131 225 4324
email: gavin.macdougall@luath.co.uk
Website: www.luath.co.uk